Rainy Day Activities

For Preschoolers

Compiled & Edited — Ann Marie Connolly and Helen Gibson

Revised Edition

Mercer Island Preschool Association
Mercer Island, Washington

Library of Congress Cataloging in Publication Data

Rainy day activities for preschoolers.

    Includes index.
    1. Creative activities and seat work. 2. Handicraft.
3. Amusements. I. Connolly, Ann Marie, 1950-   .
II. Gibson, Helen, 1948-   .
GV1229.R35 1988   649'.5   88-13562
ISBN 0-936353-00-7

Published by Mercer Island Preschool Association
          Box 464
          Mercer Island, WA 98040

Library of Congress Catalog Card Number: 88-13562

Second printing 1990

ISBN 0-936353-00-7

Contents

About Our Book

Rainy Day Activities for Preschoolers is a potpourri of traditional favorite and original ideas for celebrating life with young children. The book includes a collection of crafts, games, holiday ideas, fingerplays, adventures away from home and more. All are kid-tested by the parents and preschool teachers who make up the Mercer Island Preschool Association (MIPA), a nonprofit organization of parents and educators dedicated to enriching the lives of preschool children and their families.

This year, as it observes its 50th anniversary of serving the children of Mercer Island, Washington, and surrounding communities, MIPA includes 400 active members and a host of alumni whose children have moved on into school and out into the world.

The organization sponsors a number of enrichment classes and special events for preschoolers throughout the year. This book originated with the Rainy Day Event nearly 15 years ago. This affair, scheduled annually to provide a social reprieve during the Pacific Northwest's spring rainy season, is an indoor day of arts and crafts, entertainment and active play for preschoolers and parents.

The year she served as chairman of this favorite outing, the original editor, Delores Ledbetter, had the idea of assembling the craft ideas in a book parents could take home. The first printing of 200 sold out almost immediately.

As we now launch this eighth revised edition, we owe a debt of gratitude to Delores Ledbetter and all who have contributed over the years, sharing their time and best ideas to keep this book alive.

Proceeds from the sale of *Rainy Day Activites for Preschoolers* support the scholarship and grant programs of MIPA. Each year the organization contributes substantially to schools, daycare centers and social service agencies serving young children in the Mercer Island and surrounding Seattle area community. Tuition scholarships for preschool are given to families in need of assistance.

Whenever you see this little bear next to a craft or activity, it indicates the idea is suitable for toddlers as well as older preschoolers. Most of the projects in this book are open-ended ones. Children of any age can enjoy them. The results will differ according to the age of the child, but the process will be fun for all.

Acknowledgments

Compiled and edited by Ann Marie Connolly and Helen Gibson

Cover art, illustrations and graphic design by Jan Griggs

Contributors

    Kathy Delbecq

    Lorraine Hendrickson

    Cher Hisken

    Susan Regan

    Barb Shepard

    Mary Margaret Welch

    Judy Witmer

    Rhonda Schweinhart

Also, Irene Georvasilis (Greek New Year's Cake), Linda Fowler (camping with kids advice), Lindy Snyder (exploring nature with kids ideas), Cynthia von Suhr (framing children's art) and Julie Baltrusis, Terry Pottmeyer and Maren Tall (proofreading)

New to this revised edition is the *Fun With Science* chapter. Special thanks to Judy Witmer and Mary Margaret Welch for sharing their expertise and to Judy Witmer and Judy Konapanski for their tried and true resource material which made this addition possible.

And, a final thanks to Merle and Anne Dowd for their support and guidance in the typesetting, printing and indexing of this book.

Back cover photo by Judith Ryan.

Dedicated to parents and

preschoolers everywhere

Treasury of Basic Craft Recipes

A good finger painting experience should be a hundred
swirling adventures, each wiped out for a new one.

Cornelia Hollander

Paints

EASEL PAINT EXTENDER

  1/4 cup liquid starch
  1/4 cup liquid detergent
  1 cup powdered paint (tempera)

  Mix together and add enough water for desired consistency (about 1/4-1/2 cup). The younger the child, the thicker the paint and brushes should be. Toddlers work well with paint the consistency of heavy cream. The starch extender helps cut down on the cost of paint while the detergent aids clean-up. Store in covered containers.

  For smaller batches:

  4 parts powdered paint
  1 part liquid starch
  1 part liquid detergent
  Water, for proper consistency

CONDENSED MILK PAINT

  Mix a cup of condensed milk with drops of food coloring (to desired color). This makes glossy, bright colored paint.

  Note: Keep the artwork away from pets who find them delectable to eat!

EGG YOLK PAINT

  For each color, mix one egg yolk with 1/4 teaspoon water and lots of food coloring. Paint cookies with water color brush. Return to oven until egg has solidified.

Fingerpaints

CORNSTARCH FINGERPAINT

  1/4 cup cornstarch
  2 cups cold water
  1 Tbsp. liquid detergent
  Food coloring or powdered paint

  Add water to cornstarch and bring to a boil,

stirring constantly. Stir in detergent while mixture is warm. Keep in covered container in refrigerator. Color small batches with food coloring or powdered paint. Makes 2 cups.

FLOUR FINGERPAINT

1 cup flour
1/8 cup salt
1 1/4 cups hot water
1 1/2 cups cold water
Food coloring or powdered paint

Put flour and salt in a pan. Add cold water and beat with rotary beater until smooth. Add hot water and boil until mixture is thick. Beat again until smooth. Makes 2 cups fingerpaint.

This white fingerpaint can be kept in your refrigerator and colored as needed. To add color, mix small portions with powdered paint or food coloring. Try adding flavoring extracts (wintergreen, peppermint, orange, chocolate, etc.) to give a smell treat to your young artist. Refrigerate.

WHIPPED SNOW

2 cups *warm* water
1 cup (or more) Ivory Snow® or Flakes

Put water and soap in large bowl. Beat with electric mixer until very fluffy. Add color if desired. Can also be molded into shapes and left to dry.

LIQUID STARCH FINGERPAINT

Liquid starch
Liquid detergent
Powdered paint

Mix a bit of detergent with liquid starch and put on table top, glazed paper, cloth or whatever you are using for painting surface. Sprinkle powdered paint over starch and let your child experiment with mixing colors.

SILLY FINGERPAINT

Cold cream
Hand lotion
Chocolate pudding
Shaving cream
Vaseline®
Toothpaste

Give your child any of these to use as fingerpaint. Add food coloring or powdered paint if desired. To limit mess, paint on a cookie sheet. For big creations, use the top of a table or plastic tablecloth. Shaving cream fingerpainting can be done right in the bathtub.

Playdough and Craft Clays

UNCOOKED PLAYDOUGH
(Two types)

    3 cups flour
    1 cup salt
    1 Tbsp. oil
    1 cup water with food coloring

Mix dry ingredients. Add water and oil gradually. Add more water if too stiff; more flour if too sticky.

Let children measure and mix!

    1 cup cold water
    1 cup salt
    2 tsp. vegetable oil
    3 cups flour
    2 Tbsp. cornstarch
    Powdered paint or food color

Mix the water, salt, oil and enough powdered paint to make a bright color. Gradually work flour and cornstarch in until it is the consistency of bread dough.

COOKED PLAYDOUGH
Salt Dough
    1 cup salt
    1 cup water
    1/2 cup flour

Mix together and cook over medium heat. Remove from heat when mixture is thick and rubbery. As the mixture cools, knead enough flour in to make dough workable.

Oatmeal Dough
    1 part flour
    1 part water
    2 parts oatmeal

Mix well and knead. Cornmeal or coffee grounds in small quantities add interest and texture for the child.

Colored Dough
    1 cup flour
    1 Tbsp. vegetable oil
    1 cup water
    1/2 cup salt
    2 tsp. cream of tartar
    Food coloring

Heat, stirring constantly, until ball forms. Knead. Store in covered container or plastic bag.

CLAY PLAYDOUGH
The following recipe for playdough is about the

closest thing to modeling clay available and is a good one to try with preschoolers.

Heat to almost boiling:

1 1/2 cups water
1/2 cup salt

Remove from heat and add:

2 Tbsp. salad oil
2 Tbsp. powdered alum

Cool 5 minutes. Knead in 2-3 cups flour. Store in plastic bags at room temperature. It will last for a month or so.

BAKER'S CLAY

4 cups flour
1 cup salt
1 1/2 cups water

Combine ingredients in a bowl. Mix thoroughly with hands. Knead 4-6 minutes. Shape into ornaments or decorations using cookie cutters or hand modeling. Use a straw to cut a hole for hanging, if desired. Bake in 325° oven for 30-50 minutes or until lightly browned. When cool, paint with tempera or acrylics. Raw dough can also be colored by kneading in food coloring or powdered paints. Baked ornaments can be coated with acrylic spray for a glaze effect.

MODELING "GOOP"

2 cups salt
2/3 cup water
1 cup cornstarch
1/2 cup cold water

Stir salt and water over heat 4-5 minutes. Remove from heat. Add cornstarch and 1/2 cup cold water. Stir until smooth. Cook until thick. Store in a plastic bag. This may be used for modeling and will not crumble when dry as some modeling clay products tend to do when unfired.

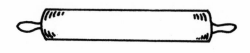

CRAFT CLAY

Combine:
1 cup cornstarch
1 1/4 cups water
2 cups baking soda (1 lb. box)

Cook until thickened to doughlike consistency. Turn mixture out on pastry board and knead. Cover with damp cloth or keep in plastic bag. Good for plaques or other "models" which can be painted when dry.

GLUE CLAY

Mix equal parts of cornstarch and flour with white craft glue. If it becomes too sticky, add a bit more cornstarch. This makes a moldable dough that hardens without baking. Sprinkle work area with cornstarch to prevent sticking. Mix up some more glue with food coloring to make a bright, thick and shining paint for coloring the molded items.

Paste and Glue

HOMEMADE PASTE

1/2 cup flour
Cold water

Add some cold water to the 1/2 cup flour until it is as thick as cream. Simmer and stir on stove for 5

minutes. Add a few drops of wintergreen or peppermint extract to give it a pleasant smell. Add a few drops of food coloring to make it pretty. Store in refrigerator in airtight container when not in use. Boiled paste lasts longer and sticks better than no-cook paste. No harm is done if child tastes this paste.

Miscellaneous Recipes

PASTA DYE

1/2 cup alcohol
Food coloring

Mix alcohol and food coloring in bowl. Add small amounts of each type of pasta to the liquid and gently mix. The larger the pasta, the longer it takes to absorb the color. Dry on newspapers covered with wax paper. Keep an assortment of dyed pasta on hand for collage material and for stringing projects (necklaces, bracelets).

Liquid Glue Ideas: Eliminate the frustration of having to constantly squeeze a bottle—and the waste and mess of dripping glue by preschoolers who like to squeeze puddles of it. Pour a little glue into a paper cup (you can even dilute it a bit with water). Cut the cup down if you wish so it isn't so tall. Let your child apply glue with a cotton swab or popsicle stick. Or, try gluesticks. They work on all paper and glitter projects.

SUPER BUBBLES

1 quart warm water
2/3 cup liquid dishwashing soap (DAWN® works
    well)
1/3 cup glycerine (from drugstore)

Mix in dishpan. For bubble makers use canning jar rings, plastic six-pack holders, coat hangers, slotted spoons. For giant bubbles take a piece of string, about 34 in. long. Feed it through two plastic straws and tie the ends together. Dip in solution, pull out carefully to hold the film of soap. Pull straws apart and wave or pull through the air.

CRYSTAL GARDEN

4 Tbsp. salt
1 Tbsp. ammonia
4 Tbsp. water
Charcoal

Break up 2-3 pieces of charcoal with a hammer and put in a shallow bowl. Mix and pour liquids and salt over it. Put drops of food coloring or inks on charcoal. After several days, crystals will grow over the charcoal. Crystal patterns will change each day. If you don't have charcoal, crumple paper towels in a bowl or dish. Pour mixture over paper towels.

EGG DYE

For each color:

1/4 tsp. food coloring
3/4 cup *hot* water
1 Tbsp. white vinegar
Hard boiled eggs

Measure liquids into bowl or cup and mix with spoon. Leave a separate spoon with each color to help limit mixing colors among bowls. Lower eggs into each color mixture. The longer they stay, the deeper the color.

HALLOWEEN FACE PAINT

(Non-toxic, washes off with soap and water)

    1 Tbsp. solid shortening
    2 Tbsp. cornstarch
    Food coloring (number of drops depends on
       desired intensity)

Mix together and store in airtight container.

PAPIER MÂCHÉ

    White flour or wallpaper paste
    Water
    Newspapers

    Mix paste using three parts water to one part flour or wallpaper paste. Mix till smooth. Tear newspaper into narrow (1 or 2 in.) strips. Tear the newspaper from the fold down. Cover the strips with papier mâché paste by pulling each strip through the paste. Or, spread the paste on each strip with a paintbrush. To cover an object with papier mâché strips, paste on a layer in one direction. Then paste on a layer in the other direction. Smooth all strips down and continue till you have four or more layers. Object to be covered may be a balloon, cottage cheese container or just a crumpled up ball of newspapers. Allow project to dry thoroughly for a couple of days, then paint. Papier mâché is great for making puppets, masks, bowls, pinatas or other art objects.

CHAPTER 2

Arts and Crafts Preschool Style

Adults should not teach children to draw;
They should learn from them.

Pablo Picasso

ARTS AND CRAFTS are wonderful activities for the preschooler. They offer new, imaginative, tactile and messy experiences. With enthusiastic help from a parent, the child can delight in the freedom of expression various mediums provide.

Ages and stages—Children go through three stages when they begin working with art materials:

Manipulative—Whenever a new medium is introduced, children enjoy messing around with it until they are comfortable.

Symbolic—Scribbles have real meaning to a three- or four-year-old child. They are a free-form symbol of "something." Gradually more realism creeps in.

Representative—This stage, around five or six years old, reflects a growing awareness of proportions and orientation.

What to say—When your child is proud of something he has created, comment on some specific detail. Maybe it's a vibrant color that really makes the picture come alive, or perhaps it's the way he drew the ears that gave his man special character. Something like, "Tell me about it" might get your child to express his feelings about his work or its content. "What is it?" should be avoided. "It" is what your child has created; and besides, can't you tell!

Take time—Some of the activities in this section require more parental supervision and help. Some can be divided into more than one step. Do the first step one day and complete the project the next. Children should not be rushed. For them, the rewards are often in the process as much as in the results.

Hang it up—There is nothing warmer in a home than children's artwork displayed. Its freshness and ingenuousness show us the scope of our children's world now and remind us all of a less complicated time in our own lives.

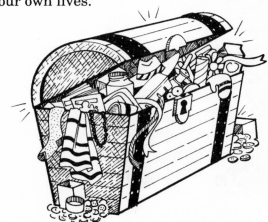

Stocking Your Art Cupboard

THINGS TO BUY

Scissors
Crepe and tissue paper
Paper tablets (unlined)
Cellophane tape, stapler
Watercolors and brushes
Tempera paint
Masking tape, craft glue or gluesticks
Crayons, felt markers, pencils, chalk
Construction paper in various colors
Newsprint (check with local newspaper)

THINGS TO SAVE

The old adage, "one man's junk, another's treasure," was never truer than when applied to the saving of cast-offs for craft projects. Even if you can't think of a good use for an item, chances are your child can.

Brown paper bags	Boxes
Buttons	Cardboard tubes
Cereal boxes	Coffee cans with lids
Corks	Egg cartons
Greeting cards	Juice can lids
Magazines	Paper plates, cups, bowls
Popsicle sticks	Sponges

Shoelaces
String
Plastic bowls, lids, bottles
Scraps of cloth, wrapping paper, yarn, ribbon
Old clothes and costume jewelry for dress-up
Old mittens, socks, gloves for puppets

ART SMOCK

2/3 yd. of oilcloth or vinyl
Bias tape
Scissors

Fold cloth in half and cut 1/2 circle neck hole large enough to slip apron over child's head. Finish neck hole with bias tape. Attach ties of bias tape on either side of apron.

SOME TODDLER ART/PLAY EQUIPMENT AND USES

EQUIPMENT	OBJECTIVES	USE
Clay	Sensory experience, tension release, experimentation, creative play.	Roll, pound, bang, pinch, squeeze. No need to "make something."
Crayons	Color recognition.Enjoyment of free activity.	Scribble, cover one color with another.
Dough (see Clay)	May lead into play with messier materials. Social and dramatic play. Tension release.	Rollers, cookie cutters, small baking tins, housekeeping play in corner. Roll, pound. squeeze.
Easel	Manipulative activity. Enjoyment of colors, mixing and identifying colors. Experimentation. Tension release.	Dip, press, paint. Need not look like anything.
Fingerpaint	Small and large muscle development. Creative play. Enjoyment of color. Experimentation. Tension release.	Use hands, arms. No design or picture necessary.
Felt Board	Enjoyment of color and texture. Sensory and imaginative experience.	Place pieces at random or in design. Tell colors, choose colors, shape, size.
Pasting, cutting, and tearing	Manipulation. Creative play. Color and texture recognition.	Paste colored paper at random or in design. Cut random shapes. Make collage.
Sand or cornmeal	Sensory experience. Solitary, parallel or social play.	Dry: sift, shake, pour. Wet: mold, smooth, dig. Pretending.

Adapted from Bellevue Community College Parent Education Chart, Preschool Equipment and Uses

Paper, Painting and Prints

RUBBINGS

Butcher paper, plain drawing paper or grocery
   bags (cut open)
Crayons, peeled
Textures: grater, leaves, ferns, sieve, string, net
   (fabric), shells, coins, sandpaper, yarn or
   miscellaneous trims, shapes cut from
   cardboard (could be representative of a special
   holiday)

Place paper over the item desired. Rub the side of
the crayon on paper. Interesting patterns can be
made by slightly shifting the paper and using
different colors.

If you use more than one item, place the items
between two sheets of paper, clipped together at
intervals all the way around. Have your child color
over the whole paper with a crayon, and watch his
eyes light up as the picture takes shape.

CRAYON-MELT PICTURE

Warming tray
Aluminum foil
Disposable rag
Peeled crayons

Rolling pin
Onionskin or stationery weight paper

Cut aluminum foil double the length of warming
tray. Fold foil to protect tray. Child draws picture on
foil. When it is complete, tray is warmed, and print is
made by pressing paper on foil and rolling over with
rolling pin. Aluminum foil should then be wiped clean
for next picture.

OLD CRAYONS AND WAX PAPER ART

Old crayons
Wax paper
Iron

Put wax paper down, wax side up. Shave, chop
finely or grate crayons onto the wax paper. Most
children really enjoy doing this! Place a second sheet
of wax paper, wax side down, on top of first (so crayon

Drawing Paper: Construction paper, newsprint, butcher paper,
grocery bags (cut open). Before your child begins an activity
with crayons or felt pens, cut various sizes and shapes out of
different kinds of paper. Children become more creative when
sizes and shapes of their drawing paper vary frequently. Good
shapes to begin with are triangles, stars, circles, long skinny
rectangles.

pieces are between) and iron (Mom must do this) until crayons are melted. Hang to dry.

"ME" PORTRAITS

Large sheet of newsprint or butcher paper
Different colored felt pens, crayons or paint

Have your child lie down on the floor on a large piece of paper. Trace around him as he is or have him assume an interesting position. Dancer? Throwing a ball? Jumping rope?

Have him fill in the details with felt markers, paint or crayons. Is his hair curly? What color are his eyes? Is he wearing stripes? Socks and shoes? Fill these in. Have him look closely at what he is wearing. When he's finished, hang his portrait on his closet or room door. If he is expecting friends, hang it on the front door to welcome them.

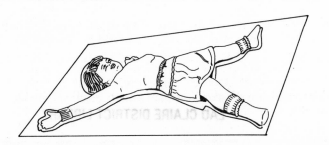

MOTION ART

Let child draw and cut out large picture of himself from paper. Have him cut it up into parts that move separately from the torso, i.e., head, legs, arms, feet, etc. Help him attach various pieces to the body with paper fasteners.

SHADOW SILHOUETTE

Construction paper
Felt marking pen

Have your child stand sideways to a wall and shine a bright light on him. His profile will make a shadow on the wall. Tape a piece of construction paper so the shadow falls on it and trace around your child's shadow profile. You or he can cut it out and mount it on a contrasting color piece of construction paper. This makes a great gift for Mom's or Dad's Day or for grandparents.

STRING PAINTING

Paper
Paint
String or heavy thread

Drop some paint on the paper and let your child make a design by dragging the string through the paint and around the paper.

PAINT THE HOUSE

In summer give your child a bucket of water and a large paintbrush. Let him paint the house, sidewalk, even the car. It's effective because what he paints changes color.

FINGERPAINTING
(See *Basic Crafts Recipes*)

No-Mess—For "no mess" fingerpaints, put a tablespoon or so of catsup and mustard in a ziplock bag. Or, put a tablespoon or so of water, oil and several drops of food coloring in a ziplock bag. Place each of the ingredients in separate places in the bag so the child can discover for himself what happens when he mixes them together. Flatten the bag to get

Water Play—A great follow-up to the fun mess of painting. Fill the sink or a small tub or pan with water. Better yet, place the child in the bathtub with a small amount of water. Try the following: Give him some implements such as sponges, egg beaters, funnels, squirt bottles, measuring cups, floating soap, corks, plastic tubing, etc. Give him a collection of things that float and things that do not.

the air out, and zip it securely. The child is ready to mix and play with no mess.

Quick Clean-up—Have any old cans of foamy shaving cream around? Give it to your three- or four-year-old with instructions on how to use it. Set him down at a table with a formica top and let him "fingerpaint." This is a super activity for bathtime too. Kids can wash the tile as well as "fingerpaint" and cleanup is minimal.

Edible paint—At snack time some afternoon, make pudding and cool. Color it if you wish with food coloring. Let your child "fingerpaint" on a formica table or countertop with the pudding, and watch his expression when he discovers that this particular paint material is edible!

SPONGE PAINTING

Any size sponge (fun to pre-cut in shapes)
Tempera paint
Clip-type clothespins

Cut desired shapes from sponge. To keep fingers clean, clip clothespin to back of sponge. Pour paint in shallow dish. Holding clothespin, dip sponge into paint. Sponge on tissue for wrapping paper, design your own cards, decorate napkins or make stationery.

FRUIT AND VEGETABLE PRINTS

Paring knife
Fresh vegetables and fruit
Ink pad or tempera paints
Colored paper

Corn on the cob—You can use a small part before it's cooked, or for a different effect, use a piece of the cob after the corn is eaten. Put a corn holder in each end and roll, like a rolling pin, on paper after the cob has been pressed on a stamp pad or lightly covered with tempera paint.

Apples—Cut in half horizontally. This will reveal a "star" design of seeds. Press on paper after stamping on an ink pad or brushing lightly with tempera paint.

Potatoes—Cut a potato (turnips will work too) in half and carve away a portion of the potato, leaving a relief design. Simple designs are best—circle, square, heart, etc. If you make letters, be sure you carve them backwards so they will print correctly.

Green peppers—These make a great shamrock design.

Lemons, oranges, grapefruit, cucumbers—These are rather juicy, so cut a slice (rather thick so it doesn't fall apart) and dip it in powdered paint; then press on paper.

PULL-A-PRINT

Styrofoam meat trays
Pencil or ballpoint pen

When doing fruit and vegetable prints, let your child experiment with different colors of paint or ink on various colors of paper. Let him discover what happens when he combines different colors on his vegetable. Keep a cup of water handy for him to wash his "brush" when he changes colors. One word of caution: It takes time and practice for a child to learn how to just stamp the vegetable and fruit instead of painting with them like a brush. Let him do it. He'll catch on with a little practice and have fun no matter what the finished product looks like.

Paint and brush
Paper
Scissors

Cut the edges off the meat tray. Then have your child draw a picture on the tray, pressing down hard with a pencil or ballpoint pen. Paint over the picture with tempera paint, and press a piece of paper over the painted surface. Rub gently and remove your print.

Variation—Use as a stencil for greeting cards.

TIE DYEING

Napkins or wrapping paper tissue
Food coloring

Put two or three different colors of food coloring into separate containers. Give your child a napkin or wrapping paper tissue and have him fold it into a square or rectangle. Have the child dip the corners of the folded napkin or tissue paper into different containers of food coloring. Unfold the napkins or paper to dry. They will have a tie dyeing effect. Try scraps of cloth, too.

INK BLOT DRAWINGS

Paper (can be pre-cut in shapes such as butterfly, heart, etc.)
Ink, thin paint or food coloring

Dropper (helpful)

Have child put a few drops of paint on the paper. Fold in half, then press with hand. Open and see the design. Experiment with different colors dropped on at the same time, being careful not to put too much paint on at once. When designs are dried, they can be mounted on construction paper and presented as gifts to relatives.

COFFEE FILTER ART

Paper coffee filters (round type)
Thin paint or food coloring
Dropper

Flatten out circular filter and let child do "color experiments" with dropping colors on the absorbent material, mixing and blending different shades.

FRAMING CHILDREN'S ART

The days when your refrigerator is plastered with colorful children's masterpieces will pass all too quickly and with them the flood of precious fingerpaintings, ingenuous drawings, etc. The time to preserve that special artwork is now.

When your child has created something you especially want to save, display it briefly for the family to enjoy, then roll it up or place between cardboard to keep it clean and untattered until you can arrange a permanent frame.

Never put masking tape on a drawing, as this is very acidic and will leave big tape marks. Avoid thumbtacks, too. Have your child sign his artwork high enough off the bottom (about 2 inches) so if it is framed, his signature will be visible.

Colorful mats are effective with children's work. Often you can find pre-cut mats that will work. Inexpensive, colorful metal frames are also good bets. While going to the expense of framing the art can seem extravagant, standard-sized frames and do-it-yourself options are available to minimize cost. And these masterpieces are truly priceless originals!

Your child can have a hand in framing his own artwork by mounting it on construction paper or a piece of sandpaper slightly larger than the picture.

Paintings and drawings can be preserved between sheets of clear contact paper or pictures can be glued to posterboard and "framed" with popsicle sticks, colorful macaroni, etc.

Drawings make wonderful gifts sure to be treasured by grandparents and other special people in a child's life. Be sure to have the child personalize the picture, "To Grandma, Christmas, 1988."

Clear lucite frames are another practical and inexpensive possibility and are perfect for a "rotating" gallery of art.

Glue and Collage

EGG CARTON BUTTERFLY

1 egg carton
Pipe cleaners
Paper
Paint

Cut off the egg carton lid. Now cut the carton in half, lengthwise. Turn one of the halves upside down and paint. Attach pipe cleaners to the head for feelers; cut wings from construction paper and decorate. Staple to the side of the carton.

Variation--You can also make ladybugs and turtles from one cup of an egg carton, or a caterpillar from a section similar to what you used for the butterfly.

YARN DRAWING

Short and long pieces of yarn

Get out the paper bag full of leftover yarn on a rainy day. Make pictures on the carpet or floor with the pieces of yarn. Make pictures on cardboard and glue yarn in place so it can be hung on the wall. Child can color in space between your designs.

TOOTHPICK DRAWINGS

Toothpicks
Glue
Construction paper
Crayons or felt pens

Let the child arrange toothpicks on paper until he is satisfied with his design. Help him glue toothpicks down, and when the glue is dry, let him fill in desired details, if any.

Gluesticks are an easy no-mess alternative for many glue projects. If using liquid craft glue, pouring a little in a small cup and letting the child dip a cotton swab in to spread the glue is a less messy alternative.

MY BOOK ABOUT ME

Old magazines
Paper
Stapler or paper fasteners (3)
Glue
Felt pens

If your child has had an experience that has made him sad or frightened and he has had difficulty coping with it, help him deal with it by developing a story about the experience. Have him look through magazines and find pictures that remind him of the experience. Then cut them out and paste them on separate pieces of paper. Write his comments about each one under the picture. When you're finished, use staples or paper fasteners to bind the book. You might even put a cover of construction paper over it and write the title on front.

Older children may want to draw pictures instead of cutting and pasting from magazines. This is really a better emotional release. It works for happy experiences as well as ones that are upsetting.

Variations—On special occasions let your child write a story about himself in connection with the occasion. For example, on Thanksgiving, he could write about all the things for which he is thankful. Or make a trip scrapbook during a vacation. Include memorabilia, postcards, photos, stories he dictates about the trip, etc.

COLORED CORNMEAL

Mix dry powdered paint with cornmeal. Provide children with plastic spoons, toothpicks or cotton swabs and small pie tins of white glue. Use toothpicks or cotton swabs to paint on construction paper with the glue. Let children sprinkle colored cornmeal over designs. Shake off excess. A variety of colors can be stored on the shelf to be used at a moment's notice. Fill an empty plastic bottle with shaker top (candy sprinkle, spice bottle, etc.) with the colored cornmeal and place paper on rimmed cookie sheet to limit spills.

Colored sand—Mix powdered paint with a fine quality white sand on large sheets of newspaper. Let children squeeze out designs with white glue (or daub it on with cotton swab) on construction paper. Turn design-side down on colored sand.

NO-MESS COLLAGE

Clear contact paper
Collage materials

Give your child a piece of clear contact paper, sticky side up. Let him press his collage materials on the contact paper. When he is finished, cover the whole thing with plastic wrap, cellophane or clear contact paper. Use this approach for making bookmarks, placemats, etc. Good gifts for grandparents!

SIMPLE COLLAGES

> Piece of cardboard or paper plates (may cut center out for "wreath")
> White craft glue or "homemade paste" (see *Basic Craft Recipes*)

Spread some glue or paste on the cardboard and let your child create a collage using some of the following: colored paper scraps; large buttons; dried beans and peas; bits of yarn; small pieces of wood; macaroni or other pasta; scraps of brightly colored cloth; breakfast cereals (they adhere easily and it won't matter if he decides to taste); crackers, raisins or spices such as cloves, chives, bay leaves, etc.

PASTA PICTURES

> Various types of pasta
> Glue
> Glue brush
> Paper plate or cardboard
> Rubbing alcohol
> Food Coloring

Dye the pasta ahead of time by mixing small amounts of alcohol (1/2 cup) with food coloring. If the color doesn't seem dark enough, add more coloring to the alcohol. Add small amounts of each type of pasta to the liquid. The larger the pasta, the longer it takes to absorb the color. The little bow ties take only a second or two. Dry on newspaper covered with wax paper. When the colored pasta is dry, your child can glue the various types and colors on a paper plate or piece of cardboard.

Variation—Use rice, unpopped corn, seeds, lentils, pinecones or other natural things for making pictures. Note: Italian markets carry large quantities of many different types of pasta which you can purchase in bulk, rather than bagged.

SHADOW BOX

> Paint
> Glue
> Plastic wrap
> Any collage materials
> Snap-off lid from a pop can
> Shallow boxes or lids from deep boxes

Paint the box. Glue any collage material you have inside. Cover the box with plastic wrap. Glue pop can snap-off lid to back for hanger. Another neat present—maybe for Grandma!!

TISSUE PAPER COLLAGE

White paper plates or heavy paper
Scraps of colored tissue paper
Glue brush
Liquid starch

Cover your table. The tissue paper fades on everything when wet. Paint the liquid starch on paper plate with a brush. Lay scraps on the coated plate in any desired design. More starch may need to be brushed on top, as a lot of tissue scraps are used.

Variation—Use heavy paper for greeting cards. Appropriate shapes could be cut from the tissue for the occasion.

SPACKLE PRINTS AND COLLAGE

Collage materials
Spackle powder
Water
Shallow container
Waxed paper

Spackling powder may be purchased at any paint or hardware store. Spackle is superior to plaster of Paris because it dries more slowly, allowing children time to make the imprints and designs. It takes 40-60 minutes to dry. Mix spackle powder with water to about the consistency of whipped cream. Be sure there are no lumps in it.

Handprints—Pour into cottage cheese carton lids and let children make handprints.

Collages: Add colored powdered paint if desired and pour into egg carton lids and let children use collage materials to make a design in the spackle.

Mix spackle with a handful of beach sand and a handful of ocean water and pour onto paper plate. Press in treasures found at the beach—driftwood, shells, seaweed, etc. Use stick to make hole near top so collage can be hung on child's wall. Remove plate when dry.

Pour into a shallow container or onto wax paper and make fossil prints with leaves, seed pods, shells or any other treasures your child finds outside.

Note: If you use cardboard containers, line with waxed paper so the finished product doesn't stick to the container. Large plastic lids, lids from cottage cheese containers, etc., make good containers.

PLAYDOUGH MOSAIC

Playdough (see *Basic Craft Recipes*)
Plastic lid, jar lid or meat tray
Dried beans, peas, macaroni, large buttons, stones, etc.

Cover the bottom of the lid with playdough. Give your toddler a handful of dried beans and peas, macaroni, etc. He will have fun pushing them into the playdough background for different effects or he will create a mosaic—toddler style.

Variation—Make animal homes. A "home for a deer"might include small pinecones, moss, twigs, small plastic deer, pebbles. A "home for a bunny" could be made with grasses, carrot tops, plastic bunny, etc. Another option for the animals would be to cut a shape out of construction paper, glue to popsicle stick and set in playdough scene. Read a book about these animals to complement the project.

Sculpture

SUGAR SCULPTURE

Sugar cubes
Styrofoam meat trays
Glue
Food coloring (optional)

Quickly dip sugar cubes into food coloring. Dry on waxed paper. Give your child a styrofoam meat tray and let him glue the sugar cubes on the tray and onto each other. (Sugar cubes can be left white for creating igloos.)

SOAP SNOW

Whip 2 cups soap flakes with 1/2 cup water to consistency of thick whipped cream. Use for "frosting" cardboard by pressing through cookie press or pastry tubes. Dip hand in water before molding with the mixture. Soap snow will dry to a porous texture and last for weeks.

TUBE SCULPTURE

Tubes from paper towels, toilet paper, wrapping
   paper
Paint
Glue (perhaps tape)

Give your child an assortment of various size tubes you've collected and let him glue them together (or tape them). After the glue is dry, he can paint his miniature city, or whatever he might have created.

Paper bag village—Use small and medium bags with square bottoms. Turn them over so the bottom

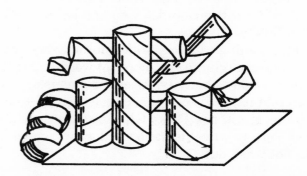

serves as the building's roof. Add windows and doors. Cut some bags off for short buildings. Or, paint a variety of small boxes and paper tubes to resemble buildings and glue them on sheet of cardboard.

WOOD SCULPTURE

Wood scraps (some lumber companies will give them free)

Glue (Tacky Glue is good for this because it is very thick and fast drying)

Sandpaper (optional)

Kids love to sand. Sanding provides some sensory experience; it provides an emotional release, and it can be a learning experience since it is one media through which you can help your child learn the concept of rough and smooth. Let him feel the rough wood before sanding and encourage him to express his thoughts and feelings. Then let him feel a piece of wood that has been sanded well and let him tell you the difference.

The sanding can be a project for one day. Making the sculpture (gluing the pieces of wood together) can be another day's activity. After the glue is dry, let your child paint his creation or color with felt pens.

Note: If you use Tacky Glue, be sure the child has a wet cloth to wipe his hands and wears a smock. It does not wash out.

STYROFOAM SCULPTURE

Save styrofoam packing materials—both large rigid pieces and the small loose pieces. When you have a good supply, set them out with toothpicks, bits of straight or crazy curled wire, small paper flags on toothpicks and any other "interesting bits" you find. Child will enjoy making "other worlds" or space sculptures by sticking small styrofoam pieces on the toothpicks and wires and then sticking them in the large styrofoam piece. The project can also be painted.

DOUGH SCULPTURE

Baker's clay recipe (see *Basic Craft Recipes*)
1 egg yolk
Muffin tin
Food coloring
Paintbrush

While your child is creating his animals, monsters or cutting shapes with a cookie cutter out of the clay dough, mix the egg yolk and 1/4 teaspoon water. Divide the mixture into several sections of a muffin tin. Add food coloring to each section and let your child paint his finished product. Bake at 300° for 2 1/2 to 3 hours. They can be sprayed with acrylic spray when cool (Moms only).

Make and Play

IMAGINARY CITY

Large sheet of paper (for more permanent city use light color oilcloth or naugahyde)

Permanent felt markers

Draw the imaginary city big enough for your child's cars and trucks to travel the streets. Tape the finished product to the floor and let him travel around the imaginary city with his cars, trucks, fire engines, school bus, etc. Draw in some of the following:

Grocery store	Street signs
Gas station	Parks
Bus stop	Lakes

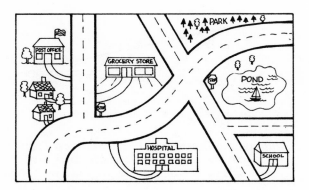

Hospital	Ponds
Race track	River
Garbage dump	Bridge
School	Train tracks
Fire station	Airport
Post office	

Variation—Make an airport or race track or farm depending upon your child's interest.

PUZZLES

Cardboard or posterboard (back of a cereal box works well)

Glue

Pictures from magazines, catalogs, greeting cards, etc.

Cut the picture into a square, rectangle or circle. Glue the picture on a piece of cardboard or posterboard which has been cut the same size. When it's dry, let your child cut the picture into pieces, creating his own puzzle. Keep your puzzles sorted in baggies so the pieces from various puzzles don't get mixed up or lost. Code back of puzzle pieces with a number or letter to keep puzzles separate.

Variation—Use blown up picture of the child or his favorite toy and glue it to thin plywood or pressboard to make a more permanent puzzle.

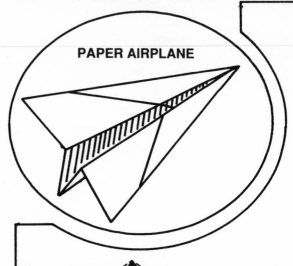

PAPER AIRPLANE

8 1/2 x 11 sheet of paper folded according to the steps diagrammed below.

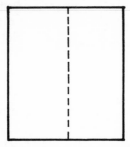

Fold in half down length of paper and then open up and lay flat again.

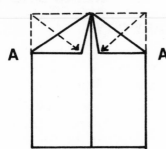

Fold top two corners into centerfold.

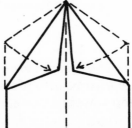

Fold points A of previous drawing towards centerfold so that edges meet along center fold.

Fold plane in half along center fold and then fold wings down each side.

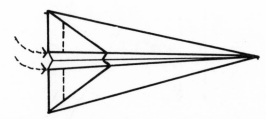

If you want it to loop, cut the tail and fold it <u>up</u> on both sides ,and it will fly upside down. Fold one side up, and one side down, and it will spin.

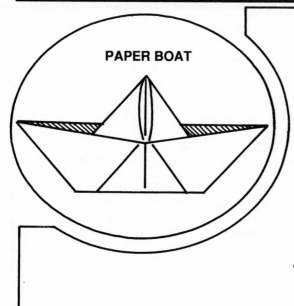

PAPER BOAT

Rectangular piece of paper, any size (if you use a full sheet of newspaper, it can become a hat!)

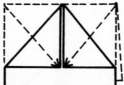

Fold in half across width, then fold down corners as shown.

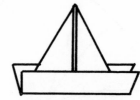

Fold up both edges, one on each side.

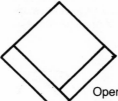

Open it up and fold it in opposite direction to form a square, as shown.

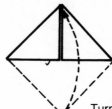

Turn up each corner.

Now pull down the corners and you'll have . . . . .

A BOAT!
With thanks to Curious George

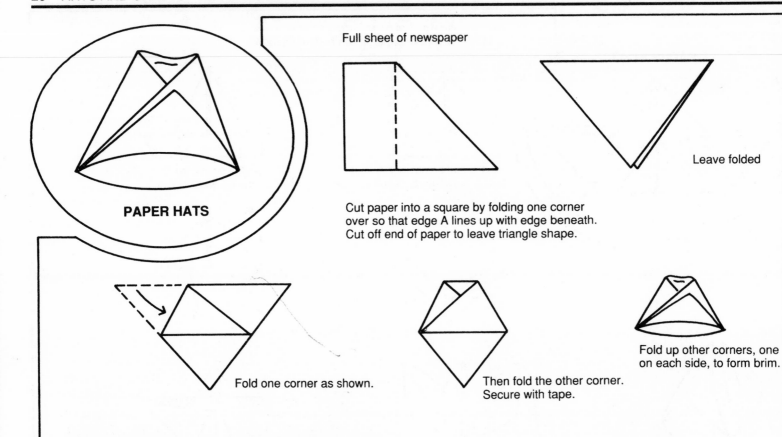

Full sheet of newspaper

PAPER HATS

Cut paper into a square by folding one corner over so that edge A lines up with edge beneath. Cut off end of paper to leave triangle shape.

Leave folded

Fold one corner as shown.

Then fold the other corner. Secure with tape.

Fold up other corners, one on each side, to form brim.

Variation—Follow directions for Paper Boats, through the fourth drawing and open it up. It becomes a Napoleon hat or a soldier's hat, depending on which way it is turned on the head. For a fireman's hat, go through the third drawing and open it up.

Stick a feather in for Robin Hood or pull down one of the brims for a baseball cap or fancy cap. What other ways can it be worn? Make one for you too!

PINWHEEL

Small, circular piece of cardboard or posterboard
Straw or wooden dowel or unsharpened pencil
Paper fastener (thumbtack, if dowel is used)
Square piece of paper
Tape

Let the child decorate the paper with crayons, felt-tip pens, sticker or paint. Mark the center of the square. Cut from each corner into the center, within an inch. Fold every other point (1, 2, 3, 4 on diagram) into the center and tape. Be sure the design is on the outside. Push paper fastener or thumbtack through the cardboard circle, then through the center of the pinwheel and into the straw or dowel. Leave enough room so the pinwheel moves freely.

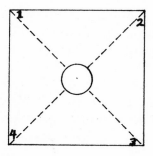

SEWING CARDS

Hooked rug backing, onion sack
Heavy tape
Yarn, string or old shoestrings

Dip the end of a piece of yarn or string in wax or nail polish to harden (about 1/2 in.), or wrap a piece of tape around one end firmly. Knot the other end.

If you use rug backing and you're also artistic, you might want to draw a simple design on with permanent ink felt marker, instructing the child to follow the outline. As he becomes more adept in using the cards, he can draw his own designs and sew them. This is a good exercise for eye-hand coordination.

Variation—Save plastic mesh produce containers and let your child create his own design with yarn or string by weaving in and out of the squares for a colorful basket.

Variation—Cut shapes out of heavy cardboard, posterboard. Holes could be punched around the edges and at intervals throughout the card. Your child might even want to draw some kind of design connecting the holes before he begins sewing.

Variation—Save your styrofoam meat trays. Find a large, blunt needle and some yarn scraps. Plastic needles work great and thread easily. By pushing the needle back through the short end of the yarn after threading, a small loop will be made to keep that unknotted end from pulling out of the needle as the kids work with it. Plastic needles are also safer to use than metal ones and push through styrofoam easily. (They are available at most places where yarn and needlework supplies are sold.) Kids can draw on a design to follow with stitchery, or it can be done free-form.

NAIL BOARD

Hammer
Board
Nails
String or colored rubber bands

If you're making a realistic design, mark on the board where the nails should go. Hammer the nails in the board. Let your child wrap the string around each nail, outlining the design or just making up his own as he goes. If he doesn't yet have the coordination to work with the string (you'll want to have several layers), let him use colored rubber bands. This is a good exercise for eye-hand coordination and also concentration.

Variation—For creative, free-form designs try a board with nails arranged in rows or in a circle so child can create his own patterns. Use collection of colorful rubber bands or string.

A younger child might enjoy just pounding golf tees into a piece of thick styrofoam (available at a lumber yard) with a small wooden mallet.

PARACHUTE

Square napkin (paper or cloth), handkerchief, or any square piece of lightweight fabric
Round Tinkertoy fitting or old-fashioned clothespin
Yarn or string, 4 pieces, each about 8 in. long

Punch a small hole in each corner of the square. Use paper reinforcement rings on a paper napkin. Knot a piece of string in each hole. Tie the ends of each string in a round Tinkertoy fitting or onto an old-fashioned clothespin. If you use clothespins, your child might enjoy painting a face or some clothes on it with felt pens.

PAPER AND CARDBOARD CARTONS

A carton big enough to sit in can become a plane, train, car, boat or barge. Remove one wall of the box for a hangar or garage. If the box is big enough to crawl into, it can be a cave, a hut or secret place. If it's big enough to stand in and the top half of one panel is removed, it turns into a store, a teller's cage, a ticket booth, a jail cell or a rocket ship. (Check with local appliance store for large cartons.)

TIN CAN STILTS

2 cans of the same size
Hammer and nail
2 pieces of string, each about as tall as child

Punch a nail hole on each side of the unopened end of the cans. Thread a string through the holes in each can. Tie knots so the string won't pull through. The knotted ends should be inside the cans. Stand on top of the cans. Pull the strings up. Hold the strings tight and walk. Experiment with taller and taller cans.

 ## MILK CARTON BOAT

1 quart milk carton
Straw
Small piece of styrofoam
Glue (waterproof cement)

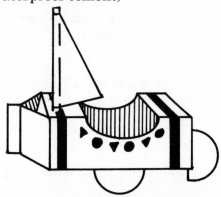

Knife
Paper
Plastic tape or scraps of contact paper

Parents, with a knife, cut a small section from your milk carton, as shown in the diagram. Save your scraps to make a rudder and keel. Glue a small piece of styrofoam inside the boat at the bottom, near the front. Punch a hole in the carton and put a straw through it and into the styrofoam. Fold and glue a piece of paper around the straw to form a sail of double thickness. Cut the sail to size after the glue dries. Cut a semi-circle from the milk carton scraps and glue it to the back of the boat. Cut another semi-circle and glue it to the bottom for the keel. Decorate with plastic tape or scraps of contact paper.

 ## PAPER BAG KITE

Paper grocery bag
Ball of kite string
Hole punch
Stapler

This simple box kite can be made in a few minutes and will fly in a light wind. First cut the bottom rectangle out of the bag, leaving an open tube. Next, fold down the top of the bag 1 inch and staple. Next, punch two holes 4 inches in from the edge of this stapled collar section. Attach 1 yard of string to both holes, connect to a roll of kite string and let 'er fly! (Markers and stickers can be used to personalize the kite before flying.)

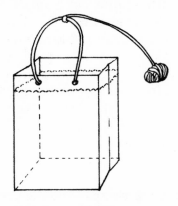

Music Makers

 **TAMBOURINE**

    2 sturdy paper plates
    Hole punch
    Yarn
    Small bells
    Glue or stapler

    Glue or staple the rims of two paper plates together. When the glue is dry, punch holes at regular intervals around the plates. Lace yarn

through the holes and add bells as you work around the rim.

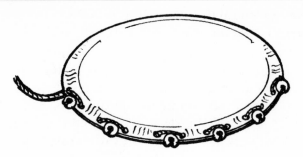

SANDPAPER BLOCKS

    Medium sandpaper, 2 squares, 4 in. x 4 in.
    Two 4-in. pieces of a 2 x 4 piece of wood
    Glue

    Glue sandpaper on blocks. Rub blocks together for an interesting sound. Blocks can also be used without sandpaper by banging together.

 RHYTHM STICKS

    2 dowels, 2 in. in diameter, 10-12 in. long
    Acrylic spray(optional)
    Paint (optional)
    Sandpaper
    Saw

    After the dowel is cut, smooth any rough edges.

Let your child paint it if he wishes. Then spray with acrylic spray (parents only) so the paint won't rub off. Hit sticks together in your "rhythm band."

SHAKERS

Plastic medicine bottles, all sizes
Soap bottles, all sizes
2 small paper plates (tape together after "noise" material is inside)
Film cans, toilet paper tubes
Tape and glue

Partially fill any of the above items with rice, beans, pennies, pebbles, old beads or anything else that will create noise. Each makes a different sound. Glue the lids on the bottles for safety. Staple the ends of the toilet paper tubes to close.

MORE SHAKERS

Small aluminum pie tart pans
Plastic spoons
Beans or macaroni
Stapler or masking tape

Fill one pie tart pan partially with dried beans or macaroni. Cover it with another pan and put a plastic spoon between them. The bowl of the spoon goes inside and the handle becomes the shaker handle. Staple or tape all the way around the rims of the pans.

Small, transparent plastic glasses
Tape

Partially fill one glass with a mixture of any of the following items: rice, rocks, beans, beads. Tape the two glasses together. Shake!

KAZOO

Paper tube (from toilet paper, paper towels, wrapping paper—different sizes make different sounds)
Waxed paper
Rubber band
Hole punch (sharp pencil will do)

Punch a hole about 1 in. from the end of the tube. Cover the end with a piece of waxed paper. Use the rubber band to hold it in place. Hum a tune into the Kazoo for strange and wonderful sounds.

STRAW HORN

Plastic straw

Flatten and crease well 2 in. of the end of a plastic straw. Cut the flattened end to a point like a "V." Blow through the cut end. Shorter straws are easier to blow and make a higher pitched sound.

CLACKER

2 lids from baby food jars
Glue (silicone is fabulous for this)
Spray paint (optional)

Spread glue around the edge of one lid. Stick the other lid on top. Let dry. Spray paint if desired. Push on the middle of the lids with your thumb and forefinger for the "clacking."

DRUM

Coffee cans (each size makes a different sound)
Plastic coffee can lids
Pencils
Spools
Dowels

Cut the bottom out of the coffee cans. Cover the can with contact paper, or let your child draw his own picture on paper to glue around the can. Glue plastic lids on each end of the can. Sharpen a pencil and glue the sharpened end into the hole in a spool for a drumstick or cut and sand a wooden dowel.

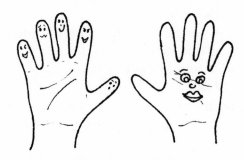

Puppets

"LIVE" PUPPETS

Washable felt pens

Draw a face on your child's hand (the palm). The face will make many amusing expressions when he moves his fingers. Or draw small faces on pads of each finger, yours or child's so puppets can have conversations with each other. This is a good game for long car rides.

SOCK OR GLOVE PUPPETS

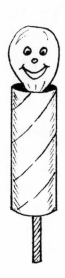

Child's old sock
Old glove
Permanent pens

Draw a face on an old sock or on fingers of an old glove. Good for entertaining kids during car trips or while waiting at appointments.

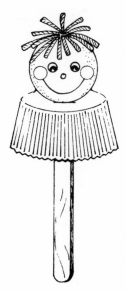

POP-UP PUPPETS

Use your imagination and your child's interests to make a pop-up puppet using the tube from toilet paper and a straw. Attach your "puppet" to one end of straw, put it inside tube and let your child pop it up by pushing up on straw. Puppet can be a ghost made from tissue, a flower which "grows" as it is pushed up, a firecracker made from strips of colored cellophane, even a "me" puppet made with a drawing or photo of your child.

STYROFOAM PUPPETS

Cupcake cups
Yarn
Felt pens
Felt scraps
Fabric scraps
Glue
Styrofoam balls, about 3 in. diameter
Popsicle sticks or small doweling

Decorate the ball using yarn for hair, felt scraps for features (or they can be drawn on). Use cupcake cups for hats or collars. Stick the popsicle stick into the ball, and if your child wants to, he can make a dress from fabric scraps.

PAPER BAG PUPPETS

Paper lunch bag	Newspaper
String	Paper
Crayons	Glue
Paper towel cardboard tube	Yarn

Use the newspaper (crumpled up) to stuff the bag. Stick the cardboard tube halfway up into the bag and tie the string at the neck. Make a face and glue onto the bag. Make hair with the yarn. (Substitute a flashlight for the cardboard tube handle. Turn it on for a glow in the dark puppet.)

Variations

Draw a face on the bag or construction paper. Cut a hole in each side of bag or 2 holes in front of construction paper, for the thumb and the little finger to fit through. Fingers act as the puppets' arms or legs. Or, cut just one hole in the front so your finger becomes the nose.

Leave the bottom of a small brown bag folded down. Draw a face on the bottom part of the bag, such that the mouth of the puppet overlaps onto the side of the bag. Glue ears, arms, hair or whatever. You might even want to glue a tongue under the fold, where the bottom overlaps onto the side of the bag. You move the puppet's mouth with your fingers over the bottom fold, inside the bag. As you open and close your hand, the puppet will open and close his mouth!

CHAPTER 3

Hurray for Holidays

I am all lighted up with lights
and there is a feast in my heart.

YOUNG AND OLD alike enjoy the special atmosphere and change of pace that holidays bring. These celebrations introduce family traditions and expand children's world view as they learn of customs observed in other homes and countries.

Holidays provide a wealth of sensory experience, with festive foods, music, games, decorations and social gatherings. Sharing these special times with young children allows adults the opportunity to "let go of the details" and enjoy the spirit of the day. These together times hold the makings of memories.

New Year's Day

Ringing in the new year with young children isn't a midnight proposition. However, the first morning of the new year might be a fun time to break out the noisemakers (see *Arts and Crafts* for homemade ideas) and party hats and celebrate how we have grown in the past year and talk about what we look forward to in the new one.

In Greece, families share a special cake with a coin hidden inside. Tradition says that the person who finds the coin in his slice will have good luck in the new year. An activity for the children today might be to decorate the first monthly calendar for the year.

GREEK COIN CAKE
(Pantespani)

    8 eggs
    1 1/2 cups sugar
    2 cups flour
    1/2 tsp. baking powder
    2 Tbsp. finely grated orange peel
    1/4 tsp. vanilla

Beat eggs and sugar at high speed until thick and fluffy. Add peel, vanilla and baking powder. Gradually add flour, beating gently. Pour into buttered 12 x 13 in. pan. Bake at 375°-400° until wooden pick inserted near center comes out clean. Cool 15 minutes in pan. Turn out on wire rack to finish cooling. Insert foil-covered coin into cake and dust top with powdered sugar. Slice a piece of cake for each family member. The person who gets the slice with the coin has good luck for the new year!

PARTY HATS

Construction paper
Markers
Stickers
Ribbon or elastic thread
Stapler or tape

Fold paper in a cone shape, staple or tape together and cut bottom edge so it is even. Decorate and use elastic thread or ribbon to hold the hats on.

COUNT THE DAYS CALENDAR

Large sheet of construction paper
Piece of typing paper
Ruler
Crayons or markers
Glue

Adult can block off calendar squares on typing paper in a calendar format, allowing the child to write in the numbers. Depending on age of child, parent may omit some numbers for child to complete or outline numbers with dots for child to connect. This helps the child learn number sequences, how to write numbers and count the days. When complete, the calendar can be glued on lower half of construction paper, and the child can decorate the top half with his own seasonal artwork. Post the calendar and continue this project each month.

Chinese New Year

The Chinese New Year is celebrated in mid-winter with parties and parades. Chinese New Year begins on the date of the first full moon between January 21 and February 19. This is because the ancient Chinese calendar is based on the moon. (Interestingly, people in Taiwan and in Chinese communities around the world observe the traditional Chinese New Year. But in China, a spring festival is celebrated at this time. For them the new year begins January 1.)

Chinese New Year is a fun time to invite children to taste a new cuisine. A simple stir-fry dish and rice or a sampling of carry-out items from a local restaurant would fill the bill. For a real adventure try mastering chopsticks. Make and exchange fortune cookies. The table could be trimmed with paper lanterns and dragons. A dragon parade throughout the house would surely banish any mid-winter doldrums!

FORTUNE COOKIES

1/4 cup flour
2 Tbsp. brown sugar
1 Tbsp. cornstarch
Dash of salt
2 Tbsp. cooking oil
1 egg white, beaten stiff
1/4 tsp. vanilla or lemon flavoring
3 Tbsp. water
8-10 paper "fortunes," make up your own

Combine flour, sugar, cornstarch and salt. Stir in oil and fold in egg white until mixture is smooth. Add flavoring and water and mix well. In a small skillet, electric frypan or on a lightly greased griddle, pour 1 tablespoon of batter, spreading it to a 3-inch circle. Cook for 4 minutes or till lightly browned; turn with spatula and cook for 1 more minute. Batter will turn from beige to brown. Remove from griddle and quickly place fortune paper in center of circle. Fold in half over the edge of a glass and then in half again.

Hold for a few seconds until cool, then place in empty egg carton to help cookie keep its shape. If cookies do not seem crisp enough, toast them in the oven at 300° for 10 minutes.

CHINESE LANTERNS

Construction paper
Scissors
Stapler or glue

Fold construction paper in half the long way. Cut from the folded edge to within 1 1/2 inches of opposite side. Make these cuts along the entire length of the paper. Unfold and form into a cylinder by joining short, uncut ends of paper together. Add a handle.

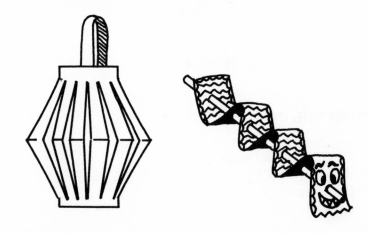

FOLD-A-PAPER DRAGON

Any stiff paper, cut in 2 in. wide strips
Hole punch
Plastic straw
Markers

Cut strips of paper and fold accordion style, every inch. Use hole punch to punch holes between folds, then thread on straw. May use marker to draw face on dragon, or use red construction paper to fashion a fiery tongue.

DRAGON PARADE

Make a scary dragon mask out of a large paper bag or box. Add a sheet and lots of friends for a Chinese dragon to parade around the block (or the house).

Valentine's Day

February 14 is the traditional day for us to share messages of love and friendship. Young children will enjoy making festive decorations as well as the exchange of valentines.

VALENTINE MOBILE OR PLACEMAT

Valentines
Hole punch
Thread
Hanger

Let your child punch holes in his special valentines. Thread and hang from hanger. Finished mobile can be hung from curtain rod.

Variation—Another way to preserve those treasured valentines is to glue them on a large piece of construction paper or cardboard, perhaps adding a few lacy paper doilies. This collage can be covered with a sheet of clear contact paper to make a placemat.

HEART PEOPLE AND ANIMALS

Red, white and pink construction paper
Scissors
Glue
Crayons

Trace and cut several sizes of hearts from 2 to 6

inches across. Older children can do this alone. Paste hearts together to make a person using large hearts for head and body, smaller ones for arms, legs, hands and feet. Add eyes, nose, mouth. These hearts can also be arranged in imaginative animal shapes.

VALENTINE MAILBOX

    Empty half-gallon milk carton
    Red construction paper, wrapping or contact
        paper
    Popsicle stick
    Glue

    Cut off top of milk carton and cover the rest with red paper. Glue popsicle stick flag trimmed with red heart to the side. Print child's name on the box. These mailboxes can be lined up around the room for a little valentine's party, and each child can deliver his own cards.

BOUQUET OF HEARTS

    Small lace paper doilies
    Red and green construction paper
    Pipe cleaners
    Glue
    Skinny vase or empty spool

    For each flower cut 2 hearts the same size to fit inside the doily. Paste them on each side of the doily

Dyeing hard-boiled eggs is a favorite Easter activity. (See *Treasury of Basic Craft Recipes* for egg dye recipe.) If the eggs are to be eaten as well as used to decorate baskets or in an egg hunt, a few safety precautions should be observed. Keep dyed eggs in refrigerator as much as possible between cooking, decorating and an egg hunt. Hard-cooked eggs should not be left at room temperature more than 3 or 4 hours before being eaten or put in refrigerator. Cracked eggs should be used the same day.

with a pipe cleaner in between to form the stem. Tiny green hearts can be glued to stem for leaves. Flowers can be placed in the hole of an empty spool (painted red) or in a skinny vase. This bouquet is pretty enough for any table and makes a lovely gift for someone special.

Easter

Easter is the oldest and most joyful of all Christian holidays, the day Christians celebrate their belief that Jesus Christ rose from the dead and in so doing, proved he was God. Easter is celebrated on a Sunday between March 22 and April 25. Festive spring attire and signs of new life—eggs, chicks, bunnies and flowers—symbolize this spring holiday.

PAPER PLATE BUNNY

1 large and 1 small white paper plate
Cotton ball
Crayons
Pink construction paper
Stapler, glue

Staple small plate to large one, forming head and body. Draw and cut out bunny ears; fasten to head. Draw bunny face. Child may also color bunny or draw on clothes. Glue cotton ball on back for tail.

 ## BREAKFAST BISCUIT BUNNIES

Pkg. of refrigerated biscuits
Currants
Maraschino cherries

Place biscuit on baking sheet, cut a second in half and place as ears on the round bunny "face." Use currants and cherries to form eyes, mouth and nose. Bake biscuits as directed on package. These are simple enough for the youngest child to help with and will be a delicious accompaniment to colorful hard-boiled eggs for Easter breakfast.

GAMES FOR EASTER

The traditional egg hunt is always a treat. Invite a neighborhood family to join in. Colorful plastic eggs filled with small candies, foil-wrapped candies or the real thing can be used. Older children might enjoy an egg relay race in which each child runs with an egg balanced on a spoon.

May Day

May Day (May 1) is a great time for a child to experience the joy of giving. Make a May basket and fill it with fresh or dried flowers and greens and leave it on a special friend's doorstep. Half the fun is trying to ring the bell, leave the basket, hide and watch the recipient's surprised expression.

MAY BASKETS

Construction paper, wallpaper or shelf paper
Large soft drink cup
Tape, glue or stapler
Fresh or dry flowers

For a cone-shaped basket, roll paper in cone shape, staple and add a handle if you wish. An alternative is to cover a large soft drink cup with fancy paper. Fill "basket" with flowers and leave it on a doorstep to brighten someone's day.

4th of July
Independence Day

This national holiday is the birthday of our country and can be celebrated in a number of ways. Since birthdays are so special to young children, you might plan a party for friends, decorate a cake and have a little rhythm band or bike parade. Use a red, white and blue theme.

BIKE PARADE

Use streamers, ribbons, balloons, paper flags to decorate trikes, bikes, big wheels, strollers, etc. Clip a stiff card (baseball cards are fine) to frame next to wheel with spring-type clothespin. Card will cause clicking sound as child rides.

PARADE HATS

Hats for the parade could include colonial tri-cornered hats (see *Arts and Crafts* for paper folding directions) and music hats. To make music hat, cut a very wide band of a large sheet of construction paper to fit child's head. Cut a musical note out of black paper or color on the band. Center this. Cut a feather plume shape or tape a real feather above the note. (This will resemble drum majorette hat.) Staple band together.

Halloween

In ancient times people believed there was a sort of war between summer and winter. They felt at summer's end, October 31, an army of winter—ghosts, goblins, witches and other wicked creatures—grew strong. The ancient Druids in Britain built huge bonfires on this night to scare the evil spirits away.

Later November 1 became the Christian holiday of All Saints Day or All Hallows' Day (hallow meaning holy). The night before became known as All Hallows' Eve or Halloween. Today we remember that people in the past felt October 31 was a time of terror, but we celebrate it as just a night to dress up in costumes and have spooky fun.

Halloween is a day children anticipate for weeks. Special projects to decorate the house make the waiting more fun. Costumes need not be store-bought or elaborate. A little one can wear a pink pajama sleeper with a paper bunny ear headband. Black leotard and tights can be trimmed with glow-in-the-dark tape for a skeleton or double as a cat costume with the addition of a black yarn tail. A plastic fireman's hat can be worn with a rain slicker and boots, and all kinds of outlandish closet finds can be put together for a clown suit.

POM POM SPIDERS

Black yarn
Pipe cleaners
Piece of
    cardboard
Scissors

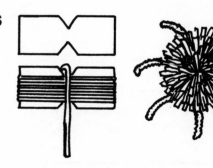

Cut a square of cardboard with 2 wedges removed. The size of your spider will depend on your pattern. Wind yarn around and around cardboard until very heavily covered. Using a small piece of yarn, tie all yarn securely at the center, cut edges and remove cardboard. Slip 3 pipe cleaners through knotted center. Trim the yarn to form a nice even ball and cut and bend pipe cleaners for legs. If desired, paste on 2 paper eyes or buy 2 googly eyes.

GHOST PUPPET

Cotton ball
Tissue paper
    or Kleenex
Rubber band
Felt pen
String

Put tissue paper or Kleenex over a cotton ball and secure under the cotton ball with a rubber band. Draw eyes on with a felt pen. Tie a string around the neck and take outside to fly. Or, use as a spooky finger puppet by hooking it over finger with a rubber band.

For Halloween trick or treating, remember that face painting is safer than wearing masks. (See Face Paint recipe in *Treasury of Basic Craft Recipes*.) Also, use fluorescent tape on Halloween costumes for visibility and have your little goblins carry flashlights and travel with an adult.

PUMPKIN

Orange and black construction paper
Scissors

Cut long strips of orange construction paper. Lay strips out like the spokes of a wheel, staple in the center. Bring opposite ends up, two at a time, and staple or glue with fast drying glue until all ends are up and you have a ball shape. With black construction paper cut triangles for eyes and nose.

Variations—Add a cone-shaped hat to make a pumpkin witch. Make 2 different size balls with black construction paper. Add triangle ears and straw or spaghetti whiskers and a tail for a scary black cat.

SPIDER WEB GAME

Take balls of cord attaching small gifts to one end of each. Hide each gift. Take each ball of cord and wind a separate path with them. Run balls over

chairs, around furniture, across rooms or outside in and among bushes and trees. A spider web effect will develop. Finish the unraveled ends near an entrance. Give each child an unattached end and let him follow his webbing strands.

TOASTED PUMPKIN SEEDS

Save the seeds from jack-o'-lantern carving. See Toasted Seeds recipe under *Recipes for Small Hands*.

ONE LITTLE, TWO LITTLE, THREE LITTLE WITCHES   (Tune: *Ten Little Indians*)

One little, two little, three little witches
Fly over haystacks, fly over ditches,
Slide down the moon without any hitches,
Hi! Ho! Halloween's here!

Stand on your head with a lop-sided wiggle,
Tickle your black cats till they giggle,
Swish through the air with a higgle-piggle,
Hi! Ho! Halloween's here!

TRICK OR TREATING

(Tune: *Frere Jacques*)

Trick or treating,
Trick or treating,
Halloween, Halloween—
All the spooks are prowling,
All the spooks are prowling,
Boo, boo, boo! Boo, boo, boo!

SONGS AND FINGERPLAYS

Learn and sing the following funny adapted songs and fingerplays for Halloween.

THE GOBLIN IN THE DARK
(Tune: *Farmer in the Dell*)

The Goblin in the dark,
The Goblin in the dark.
Hi! Ho! for Halloween,
The Goblin in the dark!

The Goblin calls a witch,
The Goblin calls a witch, etc.

The witch calls a bat
The bat calls a ghost
The ghost says BOO!
  (Make up other verses as well)

I HAD A PUMPKIN
(Tune: *Did You Ever See a Lassie?*)

Oh, I had a pumpkin, a pumpkin, a pumpkin.
Oh, I had a pumpkin, with no face at all.
With no eyes and no nose and no mouth and no
  teeth.
Oh, I had a pumpkin with no face at all.

So I made a jack-o'-lantern, jack-o'-lantern, jack-o'-lantern,
So I made a jack-o'-lantern with a big, funny face.
With big eyes and big nose and big mouth and big teeth.
So I made a jack-o'-lantern with a big funny face.

FIVE LITTLE PUMPKINS

Five little pumpkins sitting on a gate.
    (Five fingers held behind arm)
The first one said, "My, it's getting late."
    (Fingers talk to each other)
The second one said, "There's a ghost in the air."
    (Swish fingers in air)
The third one said, "I don't care!"
The fourth one said, "Let's run, let's run."
The fifth one said, "Sh, no, it's only Halloween fun."
Then whoooo went the wind.
And out went the lights
    (Clap)
And those five little pumpkins rolled out of sight.
    (Roll away)

THE PUMPKIN SONG
(Tune: *Mary Had a Little Lamb*)

We are pumpkins big and round, big and round, big and round;

We are pumpkins big and round, sitting on the ground.
See our great big shiny eyes, shiny eyes, shiny eyes;
See our great big shiny eyes, looking all around.
See our great big laughing mouths, laughing mouths, laughing mouths;
See our great big laughing mouths, smiling right at you!

FINGERPAINT GHOST

Large ghost shapes cut from black or deep purple construction paper
White fingerpaint (see recipe for Flour Fingerpaint in *Treasury of Basic Craft Recipes*

Pre-cut eye holes out of ghost or cut black circles out of construction paper to add to wet paint. Allow child to fingerpaint ghost white.
(A plastic drop cloth or old tablecloth would be a good surface for this project.)

SPIDER PAINTING

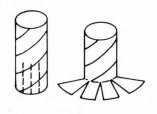

Large sheets of white,
    orange or purple con-
    struction paper
Black tempera paint
Old pie tin or flat dish
Toilet paper rolls

Adult can cut strips in toilet paper rolls to create
a spider "stamp." Children dip the rolls in paint, then
print spider shapes onto paper.

PUMPKIN MAN

Large sheets of orange and black construction
    paper
Markers, crayon
Glue

Fold orange paper in half and cut out two
pumpkin shapes. (Older children could do this
themselves.) Cut four strips of black construction
paper (2 long, 2 short). Fold strips of paper accordion-
style with long strips for legs, short for arms. Glue
strips onto pumpkin then glue second pumpkin shape
on top. Child can decorate both sides of pumpkin man
with crayons. (Encourage him to make two different
expressions.) Punch hole through stem section and
attach a string for hanging.

EDIBLE SPIDERS

Crispy rice cereal—marshmallow recipe (see
    cereal box)
8-in. square of waxed paper for each spider
4 pieces of black (or red) licorice, 6-8 in. long
Any of the following trimmings: chocolate chips,
    gumdrops, candy corn (nutritious options—
    sunflower seeds, pretzels, nuts, raisins)

Mix rice cereal, marshmallows and butter as on
cereal box recipe. Do not allow to cool completely.
Place tablespoon of cereal mixture on center of waxed
paper. Lay strands of licorice across to form legs. Top

with another tablespoon of cereal mixture and squeeze to form spider shape. Press candy or healthy snacks into body for eyes, mouth, and antenna.

PAPER PLATE MASKS

Paper plates
Craft sticks
Orange and brown fingerpaints
Construction paper (brown, green, orange, yellow)
Tape or stapler

For owl: Pre-cut round eye holes in paper plate. Cut brown triangle for top of head, cut yellow or orange eye circles and yellow triangle for beak. Paint paper plate brown and add shapes to wet paint to complete owl face. Attach to craft stick handle with tape or staples. For jack-o'-lantern: Pre-cut triangle eye holes in plate. Cut green stem and black nose and toothy grin out of construction paper. Paint paper plate orange. While paint is wet, add stem, nose, and mouth. Attach craft stick.

HANGER HANDLE MASK

Wire clothes hanger bent in circles or oval shape
Old nylon stocking
Felt shapes
Yarn, feathers, etc.

Shape clothes hanger, being careful to fold open hook end back on itself to form handle and eliminate sharp point. Cover hanger with an old top of a nylon stocking. Have child create face and hair with felt, yarn, and other trimmings.

Young children may enjoy making masks but refuse to wear them. For this reason, making masks that they can hold in front of them is often better. Stress the fun of surprise in guessing who is who.

Thanksgiving

The first Thanksgiving was a day to be thankful, a day of feasting and games shared with the Indians. The Pilgrims were thankful for a good harvest, good health, and to the Indians for teaching them how to survive in their new surroundings. Thanksgiving is much the same today. A family time for sharing and feasting. A day to be thankful.

Talk about ways you and your child feel thankful. Discuss ways people express their thankfulness—a hug, a kind word, a small gift.

PLACEMATS

Have your child go through old magazines and cut out things for which he is thankful. Let him paste them on a piece of construction paper. Cover with clear contact paper for reusable mat.

 HANDPRINT GREETING CARD OR PLACECARD

Yellow construction paper
Brown poster paint
Markers

Fold a yellow paper in half. Pour a small amount of brown poster paint into a shallow tray. Place your child's palm in the paint, lift it carefully and print on the paper. When dry, add legs, eye, wattle to make print look like a turkey. Print greeting inside or put name next to the turkey for a placecard.

PAPER PLATE TURKEY

Paper plate (brown or gold)
Construction paper
Markers

Use a brown paper plate or color one brown. Cut

feathers out of different colored construction paper. Cut out a neck and head, draw on a face. Cut out feet or use pipe cleaners.

ROOSTING APPLE TURKEY

Apple
Orange peel
Toothpicks
Construction paper
Tape

Turn apple on its side. Cut tail feathers from orange peels and attach to small end of apple with toothpicks. Make head and feet from construction paper and attach with tape.

TURKEY BREAD

Make fanciful bread (see *Recipes for Small Hands*) in turkey shape. Decorate with currants and maraschino cherries.

FINGERPLAYS

Make up your own appropriate movements to these Thanksgiving fingerplays.

Five Little Turkeys

Five little turkeys sitting by the barn door,
One ran away, and then there were four.
Run turkey, run turkey, run far away,
Soon it will be Thanksgiving Day!

Four little turkeys sitting under a tree,
One ran away and then there were three.
Run turkey, run turkey, run far away,
Soon it will be Thanksgiving Day!

Three little turkeys playing Skip to My Lou,
One ran away and then there were two.
Run turkey, run turkey, run far away,
Soon it will be Thanksgiving Day.

Two little turkeys lying in the sun,
One ran away and then there was one.
Run turkey, run turkey, run far away,
Soon it will be Thanksgiving Day!

One little turkey having no more fun,
He ran away and then there was none.
Run turkey, run turkey, run far away,
Soon it will be Thanksgiving Day!

Things To Be Thankful For

Here is a turkey, just see his tail spread.
Here is an apple, so juicy and red.
Here is a pumpkin, big and round.
Here are the leaves that drift to the ground.
For all these things, both bright and gay,
We give our thanks, on Thanksgiving Day.

Hanukkah

Hanukkah is the eight-day Festival of Lights. Each night a candle on the menorah is lit until all eight are burning. This recalls the "miracle of the lamp" when the victorious Hebrew army returned to the damaged temple to worship. They found only enough oil for the "eternal light" to burn for one day. To their surprise the oil lasted for eight days. Jewish families today exchange gifts and play games on each of the eight nights of Hanukkah.

Share your special holiday with a friend or family who is unfamiliar with Hanukkah. Serve potato latkes, play a Hanukkah game, make a dreidel. Sharing will make the holidays even more special to you and your friends.

MENORAH

Clay
9 candles

Flatten a large ball of clay into a circle. Cut the circle in half and join the halves together to form a base and a back. Place 8 candles on the base, add one at the top for the shamus.

DREIDEL

A dreidel is a four-sided top with Hebrew letters on each side. These letters begin the words that mean "A great miracle happened there."

Make a dreidel by pushing a sharpened pencil through a small square box. Or shape a dreidel out of clay or playdough and add a piece of wooden skewer. Try making one with foil. Use a sheet of aluminum foil, crinkle it into a soft ball and shape it into a dreidel. Cover it with another smaller piece of foil for a smoother look. Twist ends of foil to form handle.

Dreidel song

I have a little dreidel
I made it out of clay,
And when it's dry and ready,
Then dreidel I shall play.

Dreidel game

All you need are a dreidel and some playing pieces such as markers from another game, candy, pennies or stones. Any number of players can join in. Children sit in a circle. Each is given the same number of playing pieces—usually 10 or more. Each player puts one piece in the center. Then each player spins the dreidel in turn. The symbols on the dreidel, besides standing for the Hebrew miracle, mean four other words:

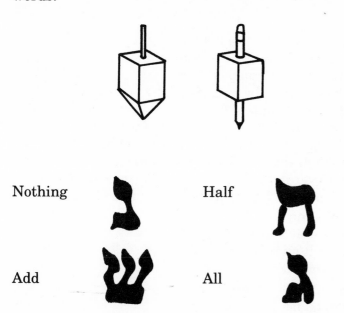

Nothing

Half

Add

All

When the dreidel stops spinning, the player follows the directions of the symbol on top of the dreidel. If the symbol is "nothing," the player passes the dreidel to the next person. "Half" means the player takes half of the pieces in the center. "Add" means the player must put a piece in the center. "All" means he takes all pieces in the center, leaving one, and the game continues.

Older preschoolers may wish to play until one has won all pieces from the other players. Younger children may just want to play for fun, with Mother adding pieces to their private piles to prevent a loser.

POTATO LATKES

    3 large potatoes (2 cups grated)
    Small onion
    2 eggs
    2 Tbsp. flour or matzah meal
    1 tsp. salt

Grate potatoes and place in bowl. Grate in onion. Add eggs, matzah meal and salt. Drain off excess liquid. Drop by spoonfuls into well oiled frying pan. Fry on both sides in hot oil. Serve with applesauce or sour cream.

Christmas

Christmas is the most festive time of the year for Christians around the world. It marks the birth of Jesus Christ nearly 2,000 years ago. Set aside a few hours each week in December so that your child can create something special to share with his family and friends. See *Giftgiving* for ideas to minimize the commercial dimension of this holiday with creative alternatives to gift buying.

Also remember that parents with preschoolers are in high tension time. Add a holiday and the times can become more stressful for both child and parent. Keep on hand many sensory activities. These are soothing and calming. Water play, playdough, baker's clay (see *Basic Recipes*) are all good ideas. A special place to mess about with stickers, holiday paper, ribbon, scissors, glitter, tissue paper and glue is a good idea too.

PLACEMATS

Have your child go through a catalog, cut out his wants and glue them on a piece of construction paper. Or cut up old greeting cards. Cover with clear contact paper. He may want to make special placemats for other family members if he knows their special wants. For a present, let him glue family photos on construction paper, then cover with clear contact paper. Grandparents will love these!

RECYCLED ART

Don't forget to save your child's artwork throughout the year for special wrapping paper from him at the holidays! Or purchase a plain calendar

and customize with child's artwork for a gift.

RUDOLPH HEADBANDS

Brown paper bag
Scissors
Red face paint

Cut a band from a brown paper bag. Fit to child's head. Trace child's handprints on paper bag, cut out and glue to headband as reindeer antlers. Put a dab of face paint on child's nose for Rudolph's "nose so bright."

CANDY HOUSES

2 empty, dry milk cartons (1/2 pint or pint size is best)
Masking tape
Styrofoam meat tray
Hershey bar, M&Ms, licorice

Chocolate chips, lifesavers
Christmas hard candy
Gumdrops, pretzels

Frosting

2 lbs. powdered sugar
2 tsp. cream of tartar
6 well-beaten egg whites

Tape cartons closed and together securely. Tape to meat tray. Mix frosting till smooth and easy to spread. Frost milk cartons and trim with variety of candies. Hershey squares can form a stone walkway. Gumdrops, M&Ms, etc., outline windows, doors, roof. Candy cane or thick pretzel makes a good chimney. This frosting dries as hard as plaster (but is edible for little nibblers).

PAPER PLATE REINDEER

Small paper plate
Nut cup
Twigs
Construction paper or felt pieces
Glue, tape, felt pens

Use small brown paper plate or paint a white one. Glue nut cup, upside down, in center for nose. Cover end with circle of red felt or construction paper. Collect twigs and tape at top for antlers. Draw in eyes, eyebrows and mouth.

PAPER PLATE WREATH

Green paper plate
Red and green tissue paper
Ribbon bow

Cut a hole in the center of the plate to form a wreath. Take red and green tissue paper and cut or tear into small pieces. Twist the paper and glue onto the plate to make wreath. Add a contrasting colored bow.

CHRISTMAS BELLS

Egg carton
Jingle bells
Yarn or string
Glue

Glitter
Paint

Cut the cups out of an egg carton. Paint or decorate with glitter as desired. Into each cup put a small jingle bell which has been tied to a 4-inch loop of yarn or string. Pull the loop through the top of the egg carton cup and knot the ends. Your child will be very proud of his bells hanging on the Christmas tree.

Variation—Styrofoam cup can be covered with foil or painted and used as bell with small jingle bell placed inside.

TRIM A TREE

Let your child choose his own small tree for his own room. You could also use branches, trimmed from your evergreen trees, set in a bucket of sand. Let him make his own decorations and have some of yours. The tree will probably be redecorated many times!

CHRISTMAS TREE CHAINS

Construction paper
Scissors
Glue or tape

Cut construction paper in strips. Start December 1 and let your child add five or 10 links to his chain each day until Christmas.

Variations

Popcorn chain—After popcorn has popped, let it stand for a few days to get stale. Otherwise it is too fragile and thus frustrating to work with. Use heavy duty thread, a large blunt needle and string the popcorn like beads.

Cranberries can be strung alone or with popcorn.

(After Christmas, decorate outdoor tree with the popcorn and cranberry strings for the birds.)

POPCORN SNOWMAN

Construction paper   Popcorn
Glue   Raisins

Cut a snowman shape out of construction paper. Give your child some glue, the snowman, a dish of popcorn and a few raisins for the features. Let him glue all the popcorn on first, then glue the raisins on top of the popcorn for the snowman's eyes, nose, mouth and buttons.

PAPER PLATE SNOWMAN

   3 small paper plates
   Felt scraps
   Glue
   Paint or felt pens
   Cotton balls (optional)
   Stapler

   Make three circles of increasing size from plates. Staple the rims of paper plates together. One plate is the head; two make the body of the snowman. If you use cotton balls, glue them on now. Make his scarf, buttons, features and hat of felt scraps. If you don't use cotton balls, paint the face with felt pens or paints, then glue on his accessories.

GREETING CARD PUZZLES

   Holiday cards
   Heavy paper, tagboard or cardboard
   Glue

   Glue cards onto heavy material. When dry, cut into puzzles.

ADVENT CALENDARS

   There are many ways to make an Advent calendar. The sky is the limit with materials.
   Felt
   Scissors
   Glue
   Magazine
   Felt pen

   Block off 25 squares on your piece of felt. Let your child cut small pictures from a magazine—flowers, candles, cookies, toys, etc. Each day your child adds a picture to his calendar.

Variations

   Sew strips of felt to form pockets. Fill each with buttons, small candy canes, small toys from his toy box or old Christmas cards. Let him take one out every day until Christmas.

   Block off 25 squares on a piece of posterboard. Write in the name of a special activity that you will do with your child that day—make cookies, help him with a collage or drawing activity. etc. The activity makes the time pass faster and lets the child know that even during this very busy time you have time for him.

   (See *Giftgiving* for more ideas for making ornaments to deck your halls or for your child to make as gifts.)

CHAPTER 4

Giftgiving

A bell is no bell till you ring it,
A song is no song till you sing it,
And love in your heart
Wasn't put there to stay
Love isn't love till you give it away!

IN A DAY WHEN the marketing of toys has become big business, there is still room, indeed, need for our children to both give and receive imaginative handmade gifts.

Nothing delights a grandparent more than a smudgy greeting card or simple gift crafted by little hands. Likewise, a lovingly designed handmade puppet or activity kit can entertain a child better and longer than the slickest commercial toy.

When a child gives a gift he has made, the gift becomes something special, an extension of himself. Most of the gift ideas here will require your help or supervision. Set aside some time to make your child's next giftgiving experience one in which he can take pride.

Learning to give—A child learns to be independent by being dependent, so receiving is a first lesson in learning how to be generous. A child can learn generosity only when he has enough for himself, not only of material things, but of love and attention from the adults around him.

Ask first—When giving a gift to a child, consider whether the gift is appropriate for the values of the child's family. For example, some parents prefer their child not play with superhero or war toys.

Alternatives to Holiday Buying

Inflation and the effects of sophisticated advertising have made for more elaborate giving each year—let's substitute more imaginative giving. Give what you can afford—not what the mass media say your children "need." Puget Sound Action for Children's Television suggests these alternatives to commercialized holiday gifts:

Consider the Gift of Time

Give something of yourself, your time and your skills.

A lesson in basic stitchery or fishing with starter kit to begin with.

Consider

Simplifying holiday meals and gifts and donating the savings to agencies helping people in need.

Create

A poem, prayer or song just for your child.
A toy, a piece of clothing, a painting or a stitchery.
Stories to read or tell or a family puppet show.

Make

A photo album of family snapshots with captions.
A book for your child "All About Me" with hand
   and foot prints, height, weight, pictures, etc.
A book "All By Myself" with drawings or magazine
   pictures of things your child can do—brush his
   teeth, bounce a ball, ride a trike, hug Daddy,
   paint a picture, etc.
A "Family Treat" of photos of your relatives
   (especially distant ones).
A scrapbook of his/her artwork, stories, poems and
   cards, mementos.
A treasure box for your child's special collections.

Arrange

A place of his *own* for treasures or playing—
   shelves, a box, a closet, floor play space, table
   space, a hiding place (bedspread over a card
   table), a large carton.

Give

An hour, a part of your day, or even a *whole day*
just to do what you and your child like to do
together.

Take

Some special walks observing sights, smells and
   sounds—along the waterfront, in the woods,
   downtown, in the rain, at a construction site.
   Don't be in a hurry!

Your child to play in the snow; to a pet shop or
   Humane Society; to a special play, film or
   sports event; to a special breakfast, lunch or
   dinner out; hiking or camping; to the train
   station or airport; to a thrift shop; to a
   museum.

Sew

Clothes for dolls.
Puppets to fit his/her hand.
Big bags to keep toys in.

Adopt

A pet from the Humane Society.

Teach your child

A trick or game you used to know.
To jump rope.
To play an instrument.
To cook something special.

To take pictures.
To sew, etc.

Frame

A picture he likes.
A photograph he likes.
A painting of his.

Renew

An old possession (new clothes for a well-loved doll).
Rebind a tattered book.
Refinish a scarred chest, etc.
Paint his room.

Organize

A neighborhood toy swap, or toy and game trade.

Visit

An elderly friend or shut-in together.
A children's hospital to take tray favors or treats you have made.

Plant

An indoor garden, a terrarium, a tree or shrub.

Build

An easel out of a cardboard box.
A playhouse out of a large furniture carton.

A dollhouse.
An outdoor piece of play equipment: swing, climber, teeter totter, sandbox, etc.

Borrow

Books, records and art prints from the library.
Films from the library.

Rent

A VCR for a movie party.

Help

A child to make some simple gifts: a potholder, scrapbook, cookies, etc.

Give

A child these free household toys: a bag of scrap wood, old remnants of yarn and fabric, a recipe file of family favorites, clothes, shoes, purses, etc., for dress-up.
A flashlight.
Plastic cup, bottles, sponges, etc., for water play or bath toys.
Sewing cards from pictures glued to cardboard or holes punched in styrofoam meat tray.
Assorted macaroni, buttons, beads, straws, etc,. for stringing.

Magnets, magnetic clips and hooks to make designs on refrigerator.

Good "creating" materials: egg cartons, styrofoam pieces, recycled paper, seeds, beans, popsicle sticks, boxes, glue, scissors, crayons, spools, hammer and nails, etc.

Activity Kits to Make for Children

KITS TO MAKE FOR CHILDREN

Kits are gifts that are gathered by parents. They contain the ingredients for a project which the child can complete or to which the child adds his imagination. Kits make great gifts for giving to special friends.

Pack kits in boxes from the grocery store and decorate them with appropriate designs. Make sure boxes are large for the additions your child will make. Add another dimension to your gift with the addition of a suitable children's book related to the theme of the activity kit.

Dancer kit—Tutu, tights, scarves, record (Nutcracker), book, slippers.

Hat box—Lots of hats: cowboy, sailor, fireman, baseball, straw, Indian headband, party hats, old hats.

Post office kit—Stamp pad and stamps, envelopes, paper, address labels, bag and hat (made from paper, cloth or old pocketbook). Christmas seals and book club stamps make good stamps for this kit. Packing box could double for mailbox if slit is cut in top.

Beauty parlor box—Curlers, combs, unbreakable mirror, hand towel, ribbons, old nail polish, bottles filled with water, etc.

Supermarket box—Cash register, play money, paper bags, empty boxes and cans with labels (opened from bottom), plastic fruit, scales.

Pirate box—Hat, sash, eye patch, jewels, spyglass (tube covered with tin foil), sea shells, treasure map, binoculars, paper sword.

Service station kit—oil can, hat, flashlight, lengths of rubber hose, sponge and bucket, credit cards, cash register, play money, tools, etc.

Circus or clown box—Tickets, crepe paper, black hat for ringmaster, crazy hat, costumes, ruffled collars, hoop for tricks, make-up for clown, book about a circus.

Doctor and/or nurse kit—Tape, cotton,

unbreakable pill bottles, bandaids, strips of sheeting for bandages, ace bandages, stethoscope, tape measure, pad and pencils.

Cooking kit—Chef's hat, child's apron, rolling pin, measuring cups, wooden spoon, cookie cutters, bowl.

Office kit—Small stapler, paper clips, rubber bands, notebook, envelopes, one-hole punch, pencil, pen, picture stamps, stamp pad, rubber stamp, tape, scissors. Pack in an old briefcase.

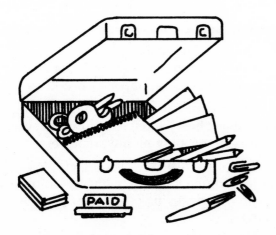

Carpentry kit—Hammer, saw, drill, measuring tape, sandpaper, nails. For younger preschoolers, give a small hammer, push pins and a piece of cork, styrofoam or wallboard for easy hammering play.

Needlepoint kit—Small square of needlepoint canvas, with simple picture or initial outlined in acrylic paint or crayon, wide yarn, masking tape to encase edges, blunt-ended large needles.

Gardening kit—Vegetable or flower seeds, peat pots, starting soil, small shovel or trowel, child's sprinkling can. Seed tape available at garden stores would be fun and easy.

Personal care kit—Make for boys and girls: shampoo, towel, brush and comb, toothpaste, toothbrush, floss, mirror, barrettes, shaving cream, razor (without blade), small bottles of after-shave or cologne.

**Beach kit**—Sand scoop and bucket, small jello molds, plastic bowls, cookie cutters, inflatable beach

ball. (Note: an inexpensive scoop and bucket can be made from an empty bleach bottle by cutting it in half, using the top half as a scoop (cap glued on) or funnel (without cap) and bottom half as bucket. A small hole an inch from the rim on each side of bucket and a cord will create a handle.)

Gifts Children Can Make and Give

PENCIL HOLDER/CATCH-ALL

Cans of various sizes
Contact paper or construction paper
Cloth tape

Cover cans with paper. Decorate with pens or collage materials if desired. Wrap together in a cluster of three or four cans using cloth tape.

HANDPRINTS

Small paper plate or meat tray
Plaster of Paris
Paper clip
Paint, if desired

Tape a paper clip in the middle to the top of a tray. Mix plaster according to package directions. It hardens fast, so work quickly. Pour into tray, almost

to top. Gently place child's hand into plaster. Have child keep fingers apart and keep them stiff. Lift hand out when plaster is "setting." Let dry thoroughly and paint, if desired.

APRON OR T-SHIRT

Plain fabric item to decorate
Fabric paints

Plain items such as aprons, T-shirts, garden gloves, potholders, or pillowcases can be delightfully personalized by using one of the many types of fabric paints available. The child can trace patterns or devise his own drawings.

MESSAGE HOLDER

    Pinch clothespin
    Small board (craft stores sell special shapes)
    Paints
    Glue

Glue a pinch clothespin to a small board. Paint the board and pin and use it for a message holder or recipe holder in the kitchen. Children can paint or stencil a simple design on the board.

DECORATED STATIONERY

    Plain stationery
    Envelopes
    Stamp pad and stamping materials
    Stickers

Stamp design or place sticker on corner of each sheet of paper. Put in box with stamps for someone special. For holiday cards, use colored construction paper. Stamping ideas: fabric daisy trim glued on thread spool, keys, buttons with design imprints, designs cut on potato, star design obtained by cutting apple crosswise, string glued in a design or small

block of wood, letters on wooden blocks for personalized stationery, ferns or flowers stamped in paint. Or even your child's fingerprints made into animal shapes make a great gift for grandparents.

MEMORY COLLAGE

    Picture frame and cardboard to fit
    Old magazines, photos, letters, lists, souvenirs,
        etc.
    Scissors
    Glue

Collect items that remind the child of the person for whom the collage is being made. It could be ticket stubs from a ball game or movie that person took him to; a candy wrapper from candy the special person likes, a pressed flower, shopping list, etc. Cut out pictures, words, and/or numbers from magazines that show some of the special person's favorite things—hobbies, foods, sports, activities, vacations, important dates, TV programs, cars, etc. Include, perhaps, some old photographs of the special person or their pets. They might be new ones as well as ones that include the child. Arrange the items on cardboard and help the child glue them. Mount in the frame when the glue is dry.

Variation—A scrapbook could be made and added to each year.

PATCHWORK FLOWERPOT

Terra cotta pot
Modge Podge type glue and brush
Scraps of colorful calico fabric, snipped in different
shapes (use pinking shears if available)

Spread glue over surface of pot and allow child to arrange fabric to overlap in patchwork design until outside of pot is completely covered. When dry, cover with coats of Modge Podge (decoupage-type glue) or spray with acrylic spray. Let child plant a small plant inside or start one from seeds. (Marigolds are a good possibility.)

POTPOURRI

Collect fresh flower petals (2 cups)
Several cinnamon sticks

1 Tbsp. cloves
1 Tbsp. allspice
Fabric netting, cut in 8-in. circles
Colorful ribbons

Collect fragrant flower petals, mix with cinnamon sticks, cloves, allspice. Leave in covered bowl for one week. Place mixture in center of net circles, gather edges and tie with ribbons. These fragrant sachets are great to tuck into drawers or closets.

CINNAMON-CLOVE ORNAMENTS

4 oz. can (approx. 1 cup) cinnamon
1 1/2 Tbsp. cloves
3/4 cup applesauce
2 Tbsp. white glue

Mix cinnamon and cloves together. Stir in applesauce and glue. Mix dough with hands until smooth. Divide into four portions and roll each to 1/4-in. thickness. Cut out shapes using cookie cutters.

The newspaper comics section makes great inexpensive gift wrap. Children's artwork is another option. A simple stamping design on shelf paper or newsprint (see *Basic Arts and Crafts*) provides a wonderful handmade wrapping for that special handcrafted gift.

Use a toothpick to make small hole in the top of ornament. Dry for several days on wire racks. Turn daily. Thread colorful ribbon through the hole. *Do not eat*!

Variation—Ornament can be used to frame a small photo of a child. Use the center of a donut cutter to make a hole in the ornament and glue the photo to "back" of ornament when dry.

CHRISTMAS PICTURE ORNAMENTS

An average size Christmas ball
Small photographs of children
Clear spray enamel
Elmer's glue
Lace, braid, ribbon, etc., for decorating

Let child pick his favorite pictures of himself. Glue pictures on ball. Glue on decorations, if desired. Grandparents will enjoy a special ornament each season, and if you keep it up each year, they will have a growth record.

Variations—A round metal juice can lid makes a suitable "frame" for a photo ornament or palette for a child's mini-painting. Glue ribbon around edge leaving a loop to hang the ornament. A magnet strip could be applied to the back of the frame for a year-round refrigerator decoration.

Gifts From the Kitchen

PEANUT BUTTER

1 1/2 cups salted peanuts
Blender or meat grinder (hand cranked)

Child can shell enough salted peanuts or you could use already shelled ones. Place the peanuts in the blender or grinder and grind to desired consistency. The grinder gives lots of exercise!

Variation—Add 1-2 tablespoons butter, honey, jam, etc.

SPICY MIXES

Save small jars (baby food jars are great) for these special recipes. Child can mix up ingredients and decorate label. For a festive lid cover, cut circle of colorful fabric or tissue paper in a circle larger than lid and tie around lid with piece of yarn or ribbon.

Orange Honey Butter—Blend 1/2 cup softened butter or margarine, 2 Tbsp. honey, 1 tsp. grated orange peel, 1/2 tsp. each coriander and ginger.

Spiced Mocha Mix—Mix 1 cup each dry non-dairy creamer and hot cocoa mix, 2/3 cup instant coffee powder, 1/2 cup sugar, 1/2 tsp. ground cinnamon, 1/2 tsp. ground nutmeg. Mix 1-2 tsp. with hot water.

Spiced Tea—Mix well 1 large jar Tang, 1 (10-oz.) jar instant tea, 1 (3 oz.) pkg. dry lemonade mix, 3 cups sugar, 1 1/2 tsp. allspice, 1 Tbsp. cinnamon, 1 tsp. cloves. Mix 1-2 tsp. with hot water.

FREEZER JAM

1 pkg. powdered or liquid pectin
Berries, fruit or grape juice

Follow recipe directions on pectin package. Many don't require cooking, and a child can do much of the work, chopping, blending, stirring.

Cards

Cards are a thoughtful reminder to friends and family that they are in your thoughts and you wish them well on a special day or any day. Handmade cards are simple and inexpensive. Construction paper or typing paper, glue, crayons or pens are all you need.

DESIGN IDEAS

Let your child draw a picture appropriate for the occasion.

Use cookie cutters to trace designs.

Recycle old cards. Cut out pictures and verses and glue on construction paper.

Use comic characters from the Sunday funnies.

Recycle wrapping paper for cards.

Dip cork, potato, etc., into paint and stamp on paper in interesting designs. Use inside for note or greeting.

If your child is too young to write his name, let him put his handprint on the card instead of his name.

CHAPTER 5

Let's Have a Party

Blow the candles out my dear,
And make your wish come true.
A very merry unbirthday to you.

Mad Hatter
Disney's *"Alice in Wonderland"*

To BE SUCCESSFUL, children's parties should be fun for parents, too. Therefore, keep the party simple, small, and of a length of time appropriate to the age group and party location. Be sure to have more activity planned than you can possibly use, rather than running out of games or toys. You want a happy party, not bedlam.

Two- to three-year-olds

No child under two really appreciates a party. For the child two to three, keep the party small. A group of well-acquainted friends of the same age is ideal. A good rule to follow is to invite the same number of guests as your child is in age (two-year-old invites two guests). A party one to one and one half hours long is plenty.

Keep refreshments simple to serve and eat and portions small. Cut-out cookies or cupcakes and ice cream bon bons which can be eaten with fingers are favorites. Lunch parties are also good at all ages since they can be held early (see Mini-Meals in *Recipes for Small Hands*). Don't hesitate to have an early morning party with just a mid-morning snack when they are little.

Have all the trucks and sturdy toys out so each child can have something to play with immediately. Little folks of two are not able to participate much in group games, although sometimes "London Bridge" (if you have one or two adults to help), modified "Hokey Pokey," or fingerplays are enjoyed (See *Games and Make Believe*).

They also enjoy playdough, story or record time, marching to music, especially with rhythm instruments, or large sheets of paper and crayons. If it is an outdoor party, the sandbox, swings, tot trikes will provide good amusement. You need not worry about keeping the two- to three-year-old busy if the materials are available for him to choose. Supervise constantly but unobtrusively if everyone is happy.

Four- to six-year-olds

Parties for four- to six-year-olds can have more

activity and can be planned ahead by parent and child. However, games where children win or lose are hard on children under five or six—they just don't understand—so keep this in mind. They do like penny, peanut and candy hunts (adapt to theme), tossing beanbags into buckets, large circle and singing games, etc. Just try to keep the active games active so that children aren't standing in line waiting for their turn. They also like a quiet activity such as cutting and/or pasting, frosting cookies, listening to stories, etc.

Rent a children's video or check one out from your local library. Serve popcorn too! Make this activity short and something they wouldn't see on TV. Many of the suggestions for twos and threes such as marching, etc., are also enjoyed by this age.

Have an activity for children to do as they arrive. Try decorating a party favor bag, a placemat, a hat, the tablecloth or cookies as a beginning activity. Or try putting out some toys or play simple singing games until everyone arrives. Six children is a good maximum number in this age group.

The Party Plan

Theme—Use your imagination and your child's ideas and interests. Consider a Strawberry Shortcake, Disney or muppet character, dinosaur or clown party. Some of these have paper plates, cups, invitations done in their themes. Anything goes!

Invitations—Use a written invitation addressed to the children. Mail or help your child deliver them. To save confusion for the mothers, include the time of arrival and departure, *your* name and phone number and whether you wish the mothers to stay. A young child can help with sticking on decorations or stamps.

Decorations—Decorate, decorate, decorate. Children love festive, bright colors and lots of them. Use streamers, banners, balloons everywhere, hats for children and party blowers. Decorate well ahead of time and have your preschooler help.

Favors—This needn't be the traditional "goodie bag" filled with candy and small toys. A helium balloon can double as a favor. Also consider a fun project where the children make an item appropriate to the theme of the party to take home. The idea is for each child to receive something special so that the birthday child doesn't receive all the gifts.

Food—Enhance the theme, decorations and color scheme. Prepare food well ahead of time. It should be easy to serve, easy to eat and served in small portions with seconds available. Your child will long remember any cake you cut up and design especially for him. Check with all parents regarding any food allergies ahead of time. This will prevent any child having to go without.

Games and activities—Adapt familiar games and activities to fit the theme, attention span, space and equipment available. Use active and quiet games. Wind down with the quiet games before eating and departure time. Have more than enough activities so that you can drop any which flops. An alternative to giving prizes is just to play for fun. Give favors to everyone at the party. Don't push. Try to develop a feel for the children's moods and needs. If they seem happy and constructive, don't structure the party— just be prepared to do so if needed. There will always be another time to use those super ideas!

Party help—Another parent or helpful teen is a lifesaver. Be sure to assign him specific tasks. Give him many jobs and make sure he knows how and when to do each *before* the party starts.

Party Themes

The sky is the limit when it comes to children's parties. Here are a few suggested themes that we have put together to get your imagination going:

Airplane Party   Balloon Party

Banana Bash
Beach Boy/Surfer Party
Circus or Clown Party
Colors/Rainbow or Numbers Party
Dinosaur Party
Get Wet Party
Hawaiian Party
Hobo Hike
Mexican Fiesta
Pirate Party
Space or Astronaut Party
Teddy Bear Picnic or Tea

AIRPLANE PARTY

Invitations—These could be in the shape of an airplane or decorate a postcard with airplane stickers. They could resemble airline tickets listing destination (child's address), flight arrival (party time) and departure time (pick up).

Food/Decorations—Hang small airplanes from threads attached to ceiling or light above table or sculpt one large airplane out of aluminum foil. Lay out a runway down the center of the table and tape Christmas tree lights along edges to twinkle.

Cut cake in shape of airplane or model one out of softened ice cream. Lunch could be finger foods served in TV trays to simulate airline food. Adult help could dress up as cabin attendants or pilots.

Favors—Visit your local airport or check with a local airline for wings, small flight bags, toy airplanes or pilot hats.

Games—Tape a large sheet of butcher paper to floor. Draw an imaginary airport with runways, control tower, parking lot, terminal. Park every airplane, truck and car your child has and let younger children free play.

Decorate and fold paper airplanes. Make a game out of having children fly these planes through a hula-hoop, or make a huge target and let children see who can successfully land his plane on the bull's eye.

An outside activity could be to set up an airplane obstacle course with clouds to fly through (sheet over a tree branch), runway (ramp to run up), refueling station (party food). Let the children fly around the yard with arms outstretched, making airplane noises.

Older children would love a visit to an aerospace museum or the airport. Treat everyone to ice cream sundaes on the way home!

BALLOON PARTY
(Good for three-year-olds)

Invitations—These can be written on white scrolls tied with ribbon to inflated balloons which in turn are tied to front door knobs of prospective guests or written on inflated balloons, then deflated and mailed.

Food/Decorations—The major item should be quantities of balloons which are blown up ahead of time, tied to sticks lining the front walk, hung on the front door and piled in heaps around the room. Children should be told to help themselves and play. One large helium balloon tied with ribbons to a basket (hot air balloon) filled with party treats or small stuffed animals is a wonderful table centerpiece.

Colored mint patties on a cake look like balloons. (This party could be combined with either a clown or circus party to help with food and game ideas.)

Favors—Balloons twisted into animal shapes, the book *The Red Balloon*, an inflated balloon filled with two or three small prizes which the children have to break to retrieve.

Games—Tie a balloon to one ankle of each child, and let them try to pop each other's balloon without getting their own balloon popped.

Play the record of *Up, Up, and Away* or *Around the World in Eighty Days*.

Have balloon races or play balloon baseball!

BANANA BASH
(A great summertime event)

Invitations—Send out banana-shaped invitations telling each child to wear yellow and to bring one banana (these will be used to make *Super Colossal Banana Split*).

Food/Decorations—Decorate with banana trees made out of green construction paper and cardboard tubes from wrapping paper. Wrap tubes in brown crepe paper streamers for trunk of tree. Attach small plastic bananas or paper ones. Use the color yellow to excess!

The focus of this party should be making a king-size banana split. Make a large serving dish by lining a piece of gutter or large PVC pipe cut in half with aluminum foil. Put ice cream down the length of the tray and peeled, sliced bananas lining sides. Cover with chocolate syrup, butterscotch, pineapple and strawberry toppings, whipped cream and cherries. Give each child a spoon and have them dig in.

Favors—Again, yellow should be the key. Stickers, crayons, banana-scented markers, fruit-shaped plastic charms. If costumes are worn, be prepared to award prizes—most imaginative, most fruitful, most yellow, until everyone gets a prize.

Games—Sing songs like *Yes, We Have No Bananas*, *Apples and Bananas*, *Row, Row, Row Your Banana*. Make "Banana top" hats with yellow construction paper in cone shapes and color the tip brown. Crown the host or birthday child "Top Banana." Throw a banana shape through the mouth of a large smiling face you've made ahead of time. Have a banana eating contest.

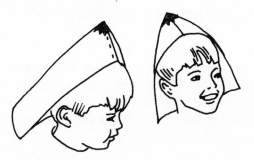

BEACH BOY/SURFER PARTY

Invitations—Make these in the shape of beach balls, flowered shorts, records or sunglasses. Specify that everyone should come dressed for the beach—bright shorts and shirts, sunglasses, sandals, crazy hats.

Food/Decorations—Decorate with beach balls, sand toys, colorful streamers and balloons.

Hot dogs, s'mores, lemonade and a cake with a water or surfer theme.

Favors—Sandbox toys, sunglasses, plastic beach balls.

Games—Play beach party music. Have a fish pond for guests to retrieve favors or treats. Do the limbo, water balloon toss, hula hoop. Skateboarding could be a possibility for older children.

CIRCUS OR CLOWN PARTY

Invitations—Clown faces or circus tents, wagons, animals are some ideas to get you started.

Food/Decorations—Make ruffs for the children. Have mirrors and make-up for painting faces (see Face Painting recipe in *Basic Craft Recipes*). Hang balloons and streamers from a chandelier in a tent shape over the table (see *Balloon Party* for additional ideas).

Favors—Make clown hand puppets for give-aways (see *Arts and Crafts*), boxes of animal crackers, wild animal or clown noses.

Games—Have tricks set up to try: walk a beam, jump through a hoop, strong man lifts weights, balls to juggle, stilts, magic tricks. Hunt for peanuts, pin the nose on the clown or toss animal crackers in a jar. Let children make clown faces out of paper plates by using sticker stars for eyes and small red balloons for noses.

COLORS, RAINBOW OR NUMBERS PARTY

Invitations—"Come to a (blue or red and purple or rainbow) party." Stick to two colors that your child loves, unless doing a rainbow theme. Request guests wear those colors.

"Come to a 4th birthday for ____" could be written in the shape of the number 4 for the numbers party.

Food/Decorations/Favors—This should be easy. All favors, food and decorations should be in the appointed colors. If giving the number party, decorate with lots of 4's—the word four, a cake in the shape of a four served with four scoops (fruit ball size) of ice cream. You can get real silly with this.

Games—Treasure hunt for a pot of gold (bucket filled with foil-wrapped coin candy); memory game with several items of the theme colors on the tray—remove one at a time and ask children to recall missing item; bingo either with colored circles to cover or numbers (for older children).

DINOSAUR PARTY

Invitations—Dinosaurs, of course!

Food/Decorations—Dinosaurs have come into their own lately, so you should have no trouble finding plates, napkins, cups, etc., at your local party store. Decorate like a jungle—use ferns and palm trees or make your own (see *Banana Bash Party*). Small plastic dinosaurs can roam the cake. Serve melon from egg hunt (see below).

Favors—Dinosaur anything!

Games—Identify the dinosaur, hide the dinosaur, decorate dinosaur-shaped cookies. Tell a story about dinosaurs and hunt for dinosaur egg. Paint a large melon the day before (don't put it in refrigerator) and hide it.

Story

A long, long, long time ago when there were no people living on this world, huge creatures roamed the earth. These creatures came in many sizes— small, big and giant ones. They were called dinosaurs. Some could fly, some could swim and many of them walked very, very slowly. Dinosaurs were a lot like birds because they laid eggs. These eggs were bright and multi-colored and very beautiful. Many were filled with a magical, delicious fruit. The exciting news is that today some of these eggs have been found here! These multi-colored beautiful eggs are hidden in different parts of town, but rumor has it there is one hidden in our backyard/house. There are clues to find this egg, so let's go find it!"

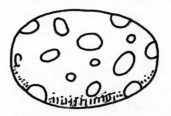

Clues

Hide clues in order—show the children the first clue, which can be a picture or word as to where next clue is located. Hide several clues, the final location being the melon (dinosaur egg).

GET WET PARTY

Invitations—A big drop of water with "_____ is having a birthday fete, so wear your suit and plan to *Get Wet!*" printed on it. You will want to add, "P.S. Bring a towel and a change of clothing too."

Food/Decorations—(See *Beach Boy/Surfer Party* for ideas), WATERmelon, SLURPies (see recipe section), LICK-m-aid, are you getting the idea? The cake could be a swimming pool or pond with little ducks or boats floating in the middle.

Favors—Bottles of bubbles, lifesavers, squirt guns, any water toy would be a good choice.

Games—Put a long piece of plastic sheeting on a sloping grassy area, keep a hose running on it and slide down. Run through a sprinkler. Set up a small plastic swimming pool for different games and/or wading.

Pool games: Toss a ring around a floating duck or boat. Underneath it is a number for a favor. Bob for apples. Make milk carton sailboats (see *Arts and Crafts*) and have races by blowing on them. Fill pool with Super Bubbles mixture (see *Basic Craft Recipes*) and fill the yard with bubbles.

HAWAIIAN PARTY

Invitations—Use pineapple, flower or other Hawaiian theme cut-outs as invitations. Or send a flower lei (plastic) with the message attached and request guests wear the lei to the party.

Food/Decorations—Cover table with a Hawaiian print cloth. Use lots of flowers (real or paper). Consider constructing a volcano centerpiece out of papier mâché (see *Basic Craft Recipes*) and filling with dry ice. Make fruit kabobs, serve tropical-flavored ice creams or sherbets and stick paper umbrellas in drink cups.

Favors and Games—Make grass skirts by attaching crepe paper streamers to string waist bands and dance the hula. Make tissue paper flowers and glue to paper headbands. Fruit-flavored treats, plastic leis, and Oriental, Samoan or Polynesian toys and trinkets.

HOBO HIKE

Invitations—Old shoe or worn-out sole.

Food/Decorations—Give each "hobo" a

bandanna handkerchief, large piece of calico or other gaily colored material, lined with waxed paper and containing a sandwich, bag of chips, brownie and boxed drink. Each bundle is tied with opposite corners in knots so that it may be carried on a stick over the shoulder.

Games—Go on a hike! This can be to a park or other picnic spot. After lunch, have a scavenger hunt: each child or team is to find a white rock, red bark, green fern, feather, etc. Make "Kick the can ice cream" (see *Recipes for Small Hands*). Then hike home.

MEXICAN FIESTA

Invitations—Make sombrero shapes. Sprinkle confetti inside envelopes so it spills out when opened.

Food/Decorations—Use turquoise blue, magenta, bright gold, bright purple, and dark orange streamers and paper flowers. Hang a pinata from the ceiling over your table until ready to use.

Serve your child's favorite Mexican dish—tacos, nachos, guacamole and chips or chili. Use place cards with children's names written in Spanish equivalents.

Favors—Jelly beans or Mexican jumping beans, straw or paper sombreros. Look in import stores for fun, inexpensive items.

Games—Mexican hat dance, Pin the Tail on the Donkey, break the pinata. Pinatas can be made from a blown-up balloon wrapped in papier mâché (see *Basic Craft Recipes*) and popped. Add streamers, paint, small balloons to decorate it.

PIRATE PARTY

Invitations—Make scrolls with burned edges or

treasure maps marked with "X" or treasure chests, pirate ships, flags, skull and crossbones. Address invitations with guests' pirate name (Bloody Bill, Pegleg Phil, Blackdog Bob). Write "Ho, ho, ho and a birthday for ____." Tell them to wear striped shirts.

Food/Decorations—Hang pirate flags, bright colored streamers, and have guests "walk the plank" to enter.

Have fish and chips, tuna sandwiches or chowder served with goldfish crackers. The cake could have a treasure chest drawn on it with candy and jelly bean jewels cascading from it.

Favors—Bright sashes, hats or bandannas, black eye patches, gold earrings, bracelets, cardboard swords, compasses and gold foil covered chocolate coins will be treasured!

Games—Make pirate hats from newspaper (see *Arts and Crafts*) and decorate with black crayons. Use grocery boxes for pirate ships.

Two children stand on a plank on the floor and use small pillows for pillow fight for seeing who steps off first. Older children may be blindfolded for this game. Try walking the plank blindfolded as long as it is not elevated.

Use treasure maps to go on a treasure hunt to find bags of pirate's gold. Make treasure chests from

shoe boxes—paint, glue and glitter.

Listen to part of *Peter Pan* or *Treasure Island* or a story from Tenggren's *Pirates, Ships and Sailors*.

SPACE OR ASTRONAUT PARTY

Invitations—Print "Blast off for a Birthday" or "Birthday Saucer" on rocket or flying saucer shaped cut-outs. Add seals and colors to decorate it. The inside can read, "Attention, Space Cadets: Report to Space Academy (your address), on (date and time). Come equipped to play space games."

Food/Decorations—Silver and gold mylar balloons come in star and moon shapes. Use a paper tablecloth and draw planet shapes for children to color. Use a red, white and blue patriotic theme.

Make space balls (see *Recipes for Small Hands*), skewered fruit stuck into a halved melon (for centerpiece) and an out-of-this-world cake where plastic spacemen or small rockets have landed.

Favors—Plan ahead for this party. A real treat to any space party is Astronaut Ice Cream—the ice cream the astronauts actually eat. It is packaged in foil and eaten through a straw because of anti-gravity. It is available at the Museum of Flight, 9404 E. Marginal Way South, Seattle, WA 98108. If you want to order it, allow one month to fill your order. Cost is $1.25/packet plus shipping. Call the museum during business hours (206) 764-5704.

Games— "Rocket ship" fingerplay (see *Games and Make Believe*) and moon walk races—these could be any type of foot races.

TEDDY BEAR PICNIC OR TEA PARTY

Invitations—Ask everyone to bring their favorite teddy bear—dressed up. Any cute teddy bear invitation will do.

Food/Decorations—Gather your child's bears and put party hats on them for a centerpiece. Use a red and white checked tablecloth for a picnic.

Small "tea" sandwiches, pastel tea cakes, graham crackers in bear shapes (found in most food stores), gummi bears and honey-flavored candies fill out this menu. Serve punch and weak tea.

Favors—Gummi bears, small teddy bears (plastic, fuzzy, stuffed), tea sets, tiny "picnic" baskets (available around Easter) filled with small butter cookies or any "bear" story book.

Games—Sing "Teddy Bear Picnic." Read or act out *The Three Bears*. Play "I'm Going on a Bear Hunt!." Rent a Winnie the Pooh, Berenstain Bears or Paddington Bear video.

CHAPTER 6

Games and Make Believe

When the first baby laughed for the first time, the laugh
broke into a thousand pieces and they all went skipping
about, and that was the beginning of fairies.

Peter Pan (1904) Act 1

EVERYONE LOVES a good game! From the earliest rounds of peek-a-boo and pat-a-cake, the toddler learns such interaction with others is fun and rewarding. Long before he verbalizes, his delight in the sing-song repetition of rhymes and simple fingerplays is evident.

As he matures, he will enjoy making up his own games. While having fun, he learns to take turns, follow the rules and share his pleasure with others.

Losing is hard—Keep in mind that not until the age of eight or more, do children learn how to lose. Losing is a hard concept for a preschooler. With this in mind, you can structure games so that everyone's achievements can be noted without a single victor emerging.

Set the pace—Youngsters four to six need guidance in playing group games. They need someone to explain the game, read directions or change activity if things are becoming too wild or dull. Don't worry about providing a lot of variety. For children, something familiar—either action, method of play or words—is often more appealing than something strange.

Taking turns—Little ones become impatient if they have to wait too long for their turn to come around. If you have a large group, divide into two or more smaller groups and allow each child a chance to participate more frequently.

I Love to Pretend

Shadow play—Turn the lights out and make shadows with a lamp and your hand(s).

Water paint—Have your child paint with water on a blackboard. He will be entertained by the designs he makes and by seeing them dry and disappear. (Or when the rainy days go away, he will love painting your home's exterior with water!)

Indoor playhouse—Use large supermarket cartons or appliance packing boxes to make a playhouse. Or use an old sheet draped over a card table (it should reach the floor). You can put in doors and windows with a marking pen, and your child's imagination will do the rest! This playhouse can be folded away until your child wants to revisit it!

Playing train—Dining room chairs or boxes can be lined up, dolls and stuffed animals can be passengers, bits of paper can represent tickets, and your little one can have a wonderful make-believe trip!

Dress-up—Children love to dress up and play make-believe. Keep an old box of dresses, hats, shoes and purses, put away for a rainy day. A long mirror helps as does a box of costume jewelry.

Robots—Make games out of chores. Wind each other up and pretend to be work robots. Play "Beat the Clock" as you pick up, using the kitchen timer. Have a 5-minute or 10-item pick up with everyone helping.

Grocery store—Use some of Mom's nonperishables to set up a little grocery store. Bits of paper for play money, a shopping list, a toy shopping cart and toy cash register complete the props!

Play school—Students can be dolls and stuffed animals.

Me 'n Mom

Rhyme-a-rhyme-a-ree, I see something you don't see, and it's the color _____. One person selects an object within everyone's sight and names the color. Others guess what he sees.

Imitate animal or machine noises—have others guess what noise is being made.

Sing or hum favorite songs/tunes and have others guess the name of the song.

Take turns saying different nursery rhymes.

Name a simple word and let child tell all the words they know that rhyme with that word.

Select an object familiar to the child and see how many parts of each they can name.

Take subjects, such as "birds," "plants," "animals," "transportation," or "flowers," and see how many names child can get under each heading.

Dot-to-Dot—Make rows of dots on paper. Use about six to eight rows of six to eight dots each. Players take turns connecting two dots either vertically or horizontally. Players should use different color pen or pencil. When a player forms the fourth side of square, he draws his mark or initial in that square. Older children see who can complete the most squares; younger children play just for fun.

Tic-Tac-Toe

Rocks, Paper, Scissors—This is played with three simple hand signs: a fist for a rock, two fingers in a V shapes for scissors and an open hand for paper. At the count of three, each player puts out a hand and makes a sign. If the signs are different, a point is scored as follows: rock wins over scissors because rocks break scissors, scissors win over paper because scissors cut paper, and paper wins over rock because paper covers rocks. If the signs are the same, there is no score.

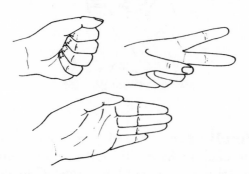

Moving Memory—One player starts by naming one object he sees while traveling. The next player says the previous object plus one of his own. The game continues by each person remembering the correct order of objects sighted.

Alphabet Game—Have your children search for letters of the alphabet (in order, A to Z) on road signs. (As children get older, specify letter must be first letter of the word on a sign.)

My Father Owns a Grocery Store—One player starts by saying, "My father owns a grocery store and in it he sells_____." He then says the item begins with the letter of his choice. The guessing continues, "peas, pears, plums, peaches, etc.," until correct item is guessed. The one who guesses correctly gets the next turn.

When the Gang's Over

ACTION GAMES

Bell Cat—Several players are blindfolded. Another player is given a bell which he must jingle at intervals. The object of the game is to catch the player with the bell.

Duck, Duck, Goose—The player who is "It" is the Goose. The other players squat in a circle and are Ducks. Goose walks around the outside of the circle, touching each player on the head. Each time Goose touches a player, Goose says, "Duck." But if Goose touches a player's head and says, "Goose," that player jumps up and chases Goose around the Circle. If Goose reaches the player's place before being tagged, the player becomes the next Goose. If Goose is tagged, Goose is "It" again.

Drop the Handkerchief—One player is "It." The other players sit in a circle and put their hands behind them. "It" has a handkerchief and skips around the circle as everybody sings:

A tisket, a tasket,
A green and yellow basket,
I sent a letter to my love
And on the way I dropped it,
I dropped it, I dropped it.

"It" drops the handkerchief into a player's hands and starts to run. The player must run in the opposite direction. The first to reach the empty place sits down. The other player is "It."

Simon Says—One player chosen to be Simon, takes his place before the others. He commands some movement, such as, "Simon says bend your knees" or "sit down." If he omits "Simon says" before his command, the players should not do the movement even though Simon does. If players make movement,

they must be seated, and last player standing before Simon is the next Simon.

Ring Around the Rosy—The children walk or skip in a circle, holding hands and singing:

Ring around a rosy,
A pocketful of posies,
One, two and three,
We all fall down.
    (And down to the floor they go.)

London Bridge—Two players are chosen to be a bridge and each picks a different symbol—silver slipper, pearl necklace, golden arrow. They clasp each other's hands, raising their arms in the air so the other children walk underneath. When the game starts, the other players form a line and march under the bridge singing:

London Bridge is falling down,
Falling down, falling down,
London bridge is falling down,
My fair lady!

On the word "lady" the bridge catches the player going under and swings him back and forth singing:

Take the keys and lock him up,
Lock him up, lock him up,
Take the keys and lock him up,
My fair lady.

They take the prisoner off to a corner to choose between the two symbols they have chosen. The prisoner stands behind the child whose symbol he chooses. Game continues till all have been caught. Then the teams have a tug of war.

Farmer in the Dell—One player is chosen to be the farmer. The others join hands and form a circle around the farmer. They skip around the farmer singing:

The farmer in the dell,
The farmer in the dell,
Heigh-ho, the derry-o,
The farmer in the dell.

The farmer picks a player to be the wife. This player joins the farmer in the circle. The others continue to skip around them singing:

The farmer takes a wife,
The farmer takes a wife,
Heigh-ho, the derry-o,
The farmer takes a wife.

After each verse, the last player to enter the circle selects the next to come in. Remaining verses are:

The wife picks a child . . . the child picks a nurse . . . The nurse picks a dog . . . the dog picks a cat . . . the cat picks a rat . . .the rat picks the cheese.

When the cheese is chosen, all players clap their hands and skip around the cheese, singing:

The cheese stands alone,
The cheese stands alone,
Heigh-ho, the derry-o,
The cheese stands alone.

The cheese becomes the farmer if the game is played again.

Follow the leader—One person starts the game, with other players taking a turn in order. The first person does one simple motion (i.e., clap hands, salute, shake head, etc.). The next player must repeat the motion and then add one more movement. The game continues by remembering the correct order of motions.

Touch Blue—Have children stand in open space. Start by asking them to touch something blue on anyone or anything. Then quickly give them more instructions (i.e., touch shoes, touch a button, etc.). This is a quick, fun ice-breaker at a party, too.

Zoom—Players stand in a circle facing center. "Zoom" is the sound of a racing car; "Eek" is the sound of slammed brakes. The first person starts by saying, "Zoom," and quickly turning his head toward the person next to him, who quickly turns his head and says, "Zoom," to the next player and so on going rapidly around the circle. At any point a player can say, "Eek," instead of "Zoom," in which case the "Zoom" goes around the circle in the opposite direction.

Mother, May I—One child is designated Mother (Father). All other children line up across room facing Mother. Mother gives a direction, such as "Take two giant steps," or "Take three tiny hops." Children must ask Mother, "Mother, may I?" and be answered, "Yes, you may," before they may move. If they move without first asking, they must return to end of room to start again (younger children could just stay in place and miss that turn). First one to reach Mother gets to be Mother in next round.

Poor Kitty—One player is chosen to be Kitty. The other players sit in a circle with Kitty in the center. Kitty crawls around the circle. Every time Kitty stops in front of someone, that player must stroke Kitty's hair, look him or her in the face, and say, "Poor Kitty," three times without smiling. Kitty, acting like a kitten, tries to make the player laugh or smile. If Kitty fails to do so, he moves to the next player. The first person to laugh becomes the next Kitty. No tickling allowed!

Three Legged Race—Have two children stand side by side. Tie their inside shoes, ankles or legs together, creating three movable legs. Let them race each other (or they'll have lots of fun just walking around!). For safety's sake, use only one level of your house.

Hot and Cold—After one player is sent out of the room, the other players select an object for him to guess. The absent player is called back, and he must move about the room trying to guess the object. When he is far away from it, the other players say, "Cold." As he gets nearer, they say, "Warm" and "Warmer," and when he is very near, they say, "Hot." The player has three chances to guess the object, so it is best to wait until he hears "Hot." All players take a turn.

FUN FOR PARTIES

Place three to five objects (comb, button, etc.) on a tray. Place in a row and have children name each object. Have them close their eyes while you take away an object and/or rearrange the remaining ones. Have them name the missing object or put objects back in their original order.

Drop clothespins into milk bottles or throw clothespins into a large pan. Toss Ping Pong balls into empty egg cartons or large tin can. Toss Nerf ball (or balls made from crumpling up newspaper) into a wastebasket.

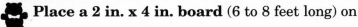 **Place a 2 in. x 4 in. board** (6 to 8 feet long) on

the floor, or lay down a strip of masking tape and let the children walk on it, practicing their balance. (Or if you're having a circus theme party, pretend it is the high wire in the circus).

Broken Stars—Color one dark and one white star, cut each into sections and then hide each section. Divide children into two groups, having one group find and put together the dark star and the other group the white star. The group finishing first can win a prize, or everyone gets prize for finishing.

Variation—Buy poster size dinosaurs, storybook characters or whatever your theme, glue onto cardboard and cut.

Pass the Nickel—A nickel is given to one player in the circle and passed around among the players while music is played. When the music stops, the child who has the nickel drops out. Younger children can remain in the circle or sit in the middle if sitting out is too hard.

Pin Petals on daisies, tails on donkeys or nose on clown. (Scotch tape instead of pins.) Variation for Halloween—Tail or whiskers on a black cat. Blindfold the child and spin him around three times.

Bowling—Knock down objects (empty plastic bottles or milk cartons work well) with a ball. Prizes could be numbered and the child wins the one that matches the number of pins knocked down.

The Indian or Pirate Trail—Take balls of cord attaching small gifts to one end of each. Place these gifts in hidden places. Take each ball of cord and wind a separate trail with it. Run it over chairs, around furniture, across rooms. Have the trails cross each other and wind up in a spider web effect. Finish trails near entrance. Give each child an unattached end and let him follow his trail. Can be a Halloween game with the spider web created.

Zoo—Hide peanuts in the shell around the room. Have children choose what zoo animal they want to be. Have them find the hidden peanuts making the appropriate animal sound before they pick up the peanut. Beware of choking danger with younger preschoolers.

Spin a Stunt—Draw 12 in. diameter circle on a piece of cardboard. Divide it into pie-shaped pieces, making one piece or more for each person playing. Cut arrow (spinner) out of cardboard or plastic and attach it to center of circle with paper fastener. Ask each child to name a stunt or action (jump, whistle, beat chest, etc.) and write each idea on each pie piece. Children take turns spinning arrow, and all children join in doing the action. You'll get a variety of crazy stunts and lots of laughing kids.

Musical Chairs Variation—For younger children, this game can be "Share the Chair" (or try pillows). After each turn, one chair/pillow is removed, and the challenge is to see how many can fit on the remaining chairs/pillows.

Colored Stone Stepping—Cut out large pieces of colored paper in any shape to use as "stone." Place around room on the floor like stones in a shallow pond. Call out colors as children are to step from one to another without stepping off into the pond.

Beanbag Toss—Place various colored carpet samples on the floor a short distance from where the child is standing. Instruct child to toss the beanbag to "hit the red square," etc.

Cover Up—Place a large coin or poker chip in a bucket and fill the bucket with 6 in. to 8 in. of water. Divide about 15 pennies among the players and let each take a turn dropping pennies into the bucket, trying to cover the larger coin completely. If the group does it before they run out of pennies, they win. If not, the bucket wins and they try again. (Note: Beware of choking danger with young preschoolers.)

CARD GAMES

War—No limit to number of players. Two decks

may be used. Deal all cards; players stack cards face down. Player to right of dealer turns top card over, and each player following turns up top card. High card wins and takes other cards by saying, for example, "My 10 takes your 3, and your 6." Winner turns the next top card and starts the next round. If two or more players turn the same card, there is war. Players in the war place three cards from their stack face down and turn the fourth card up. Winner of the war (highest fourth card) takes all the cards.

Royal Family—Deal out a deck of cards evenly. Put face down in a stack. Parent/leader says, "Start." Each player turns over a card. If the card is a King, everyone must nod their heads; Queen, bow with hands together; Jack, slap the table. The last person to make the gesture must take all the cards. The person with the least number of cards wins.

Old Maid—Use a regular deck of cards with one joker, or buy an Old Maid deck. Deal out deck of cards to all players. Players match as many pairs as possible in their hand and put them face down on the table. The starting player draws a card from another player. If it matches a card in his hand, he lays the pair down. The game proceeds until all pairs are matched, leaving the Old Maid in one player's hand (the loser).

Fish—If there are two players, each one gets seven cards. If more than two players, each one gets five cards. The leftover cards are placed in the middle of the table for "fishing."

First player pulls all pairs out of his hand and places them on the table. Then he asks any other player for a card to match one in his hand. If the other has that card, he hands it over, the player places the pair on the table and gets another turn. If the other player doesn't have the card, he tells the player, "Go fish," and the player must pick up a card from the center pile (a matched pair may be placed on the table, and then the player's turn is ended). The first player out of cards (or the one with the most matched pairs) wins.

Slap Jack—Deal out all cards. Each player places his cards in a pile face down in front of him. Player on dealer's left begins by turning over his top card and placing it in the center. Play continues clockwise. Each time a Jack is played, the players reach out to slap it. The first player to do so (player whose hand is directly on top of it) gets the pile of cards in the center, which he shuffles face down with those in front of him. If a player mistakenly slaps a card (not a Jack), he must give a card to the player who put the card in the center. When a player loses all of his cards, he may wait until one more Jack is played and try to win the center cards—if he does not, he is out of the game. Player who has all the cards wins.

Concentration—Sort through deck of cards and pull out three to 10 pairs (depending on age of child). Shuffle them and place them face down in rows. Each player, in turn, turns over two cards. If they match, he keeps them and takes another turn. If not, they are placed face down in their original spots. Player with most matched pairs is winner or could be called a "good rememberer." You can make your own cards by cutting out pictures from magazines and gluing them on 3 in. x 5 in. cards.

Fingerplays

THE WHEELS ON THE BUS

The wheels on the bus go round and round
Round and round, round and round.
The wheels on the bus go round and round,
All day long.
(Make hands go r ound like tires)

Continue to add to the song: the horn on the bus, honk-honk-honk; the windshield wiper, swish-swish-swish; the driver on the bus says move on back, move on back, move on back; the baby, waa-waa-waa; the mommy, don't cry now, don't cry now, etc. (Mime the actions suggested by the words.)

EENSY WEENSY SPIDER

The eensy, weensy spider climbed up the water spout;
Down came the rain and washed the spider out.
Out came the sun and dried up all the rain,
And the eensy, weensy spider climbed up the spout again.
(Mime the actions suggested by the words.)

IF YOU'RE HAPPY AND YOU KNOW IT

If you're happy and you know it, clap your hands.
(clap, clap)

If you're happy and you know it, clap your hands.
  (clap, clap)
If you're happy and you know it, then you really
  ought to show it,
If you're happy and you know it, clap your hands.
  (clap, clap)

Other verses

Touch your nose
Show a smile
Tap your knees
Sing really loud
Sing really soft
Turn around
Stamp your feet

FIVE LITTLE MONKEYS

Five little monkeys bouncing on the bed
  (Let fingers of one hand bounce on other)
One fell off and bumped his head.
  (Hold head)
Mama called the doctor and the doctor said,
  (Dialing motions)
"No more monkeys bouncing on the bed."
  (Shake a finger)
Four little monkeys bouncing on the bed, etc.

PETER HAMMERS

Peter hammers with one hammer, one hammer,
  one hammer,
  (Pound one fist on floor or leg)
Peter hammers with one hammer all day long.
Two hammers (two fists)
Three hammers (two fists, one foot)
Four hammers (two fists, two feet)
Five hammers (two fists, two feet, head)
Peter's very tired now (rub eyes, then lay head on
  hands)

JACK-IN-THE-BOX

Jack-in-the-box shut up so tight
  (Curl up tightly on floor)
Down in the dark without any light.
  (Tuck head down)
Jack-in-the-box you sit so still
  (Freeze)
Won't you come out?
Yes, you will!
  (Fling arms and pop out)

DON'T TOUCH THE BABY

(Child holds up hand, fingers outstretched;
  points to each finger as he playfully sings:)

Mother, Father, Sister, Brother—but don't touch
   the Baby!
   (Doesn't touch little finger)
   (Repeat several times, then—)
Mother, Father, Sister, Brother, Waa—I touched
   the Baby!

TEDDY BEAR

Teddy bear, teddy bear, turn around.
Teddy bear, teddy bear, touch the ground.
Teddy bear, teddy bear, turn out the light.
Teddy bear, teddy bear, say "Good night."
   (Act out the motions)

FIVE LITTLE FRECKLED FROGS

Five little freckled frogs,
   (Five fingers up with your other arm as log)
Sitting on a speckled log,
Eating the most delicious bugs,
Yum, yum!
   (Rub tummy)
One jumped into the pool,
   (One finger jumps off log and disappears)
Where it was nice and cool.
Now there are four little freckled frogs!
   (Continue on down to one frog)

ROW YOUR BOAT

   (Adult and child sit on floor facing each other.
   Soles of adult's feet rest against soles of
   child's feet. Hold hands with each other.
   Sing *Row, Row, Row Your Boat*. Lean back
   and pull child towards you; then let child
   pull you. Do in rhythm as you sing song.)
Row, row, row your boat
Gently down the stream.
Merrily, merrily, merrily, merrily,
Life is but a dream!

WHERE IS THUMBKIN?
(Tune: *Frere Jacques*)

Where is Thumbkin? Where is Thumbkin?
Here I am
   (Hold up one thumb)
Here I am
   (Other thumb)
How are you today, Sir?
   (Wiggle one thumb at the other)
Very fine, I thank you.
Run away, run away
   (Hide behind back)

Do the same movements with Pointer, Tall Man,
Ring Man and Pinky.

WALK WITH TEDDY BEAR

Walking around the garden
With my Teddy Bear
    (Child holds out palm, adult uses two of her
       fingers to walk around on it)
One step, two step
    (Fingers walk up child's arm)
Ticklish under there!
    (Tickle under arm)

CREEPING MOUSEY

See the little mousey
Creeping up the stairs
    (Adult uses two fingers to creep up
       outstretched arm of child)
Looking for a warm nest
There, oh, there!
    (Tickle under chin)

TWO LITTLE BLACKBIRDS

Two little blackbirds sitting on a hill
    (Place forefinger of each hand on shoulder)
One named Jack
    (Hold one finger out)
The other named Jill.
    (Hold out other finger)

Fly away Jack, fly away Jill!
    (Make one hand and then the other "fly away")
Come back Jack, come back Jill!
    (Bring hands back to shoulders one at a time)

OPEN THEM, SHUT THEM

Open them, shut them
Open them, shut them
Give a little clap.
Open them, shut them
Open them, shut them
Lay them in your lap.
    (Do appropriate motions)

THE BEE

What do you suppose?
A bee sat on my nose.
    (Land the tips of finger and thumb, touching,
       on bridge of nose)
Then what do you think?
He gave me a wink
    (Wink one eye)
And said, "I beg your pardon,
I thought you were my garden!"
    (Make flying-away movements with hand)

HERE IS THE BEEHIVE

Here is the beehive.
(Make a beehive with two hands, fingers
interlocked)
Where are the bees?
Hiding where nobody sees.
Watch them come creeping
(Creep the fingers of one hand out of the other,
then make them fly about)
Out of their hive;
One and two and three, four, five.

FIVE LITTLE PEAS

Five little peas in a pea-pod pressed,
(Clench fingers on one hand)
One grew, two grew and so did all the rest.
(Raise fingers slowly)
They grew and grew and did not stop
(Stretch fingers wide)
Until one day the pod went POP!
(Clap loudly on POP)

I'M A LITTLE TEAPOT

I'm a little teapot, short and stout,
Here is my handle, here is my spout.
(Put one hand on hip, hold out the other arm
as spout)

When I get all steamed up, hear me shout,
Tip me over and pour me out.
(Tip slowly to the side of the outstretched arm)

TEN LITTLE FINGERS

I have 10 little fingers
And they all belong to me.
I can make them do things

Would you like to see?
I can shut them up tight
I can open them wide.
I can put them together
I can make them all hide.
I can make them jump high
I can make them jump low.
I can fold them up quietly
And hold them just so.
(Make appropriate motions)

SKIDAMARINK

Skidamarink -a-dink-a-dink
(Right elbow in left hand, wiggle fingers)
Skidamarink-a-doo
(Repeat, only opposite)
I love you.
(Point to self, hug self, point to other person)
Skidamarink-a-dink-a-dink
(Same as above)
Skidamarink-a-doo
I love you.

I love you in the morning
(Hands locked high above head)
And in the afternoon
(Lower to shoulder level)
I love you in the evening

(Lower to hip level)
And underneath the moon.
(Arms make big circle overhead)
Oh, skidamarink-a-dink-a-dink
(Same as above)
I love you (I love you).

LITTLE CABIN IN THE WOOD

Little cabin in the wood,
(Form a peaked roof with fingertips touching)
Little man by the window stood,
(Shade eyes, peer out window)
Little rabbit hopping by,
(Middle and forefingers up, make rabbit hop)
Knocking at the door.
(Knock)
"Help me! Help me, sir!
(Wave hands)
" 'fore the farmer bops my head."
(Knock head)
"Come on in," the little man cried
(Beckon rabbit)
"Warm up by the fire."

NOBLE DUKE OF YORK

(Adult sits on floor with legs out straight.
Child sits on your knees and holds adult's
hands.)

The Noble Duke of York
    (Bounce knees in rhythm)
He had ten thousand men.
He marched them up the hill
    (Raise knees up)
And he marched them down again.
    (Knees down)
And when they were up, they were up
    (Knees up)
And when they were down, they were down
    (Knees down)
And when they were only halfway up
    (Knees halfway up)
They were neither up nor down.
    (Knees up and down quickly)

DO YOUR EARS HANG LOW?
(Tune: *Turkey in the Straw*)

Do your ears hang low?
    (Hands upside down, wrists against ears,
      wiggle)
Do they wobble to and fro?
Can you tie them in a knot?
Can you tie them in a bow?
    (Make motion of tying bow)

Can you throw them over your shoulder like a
    Continental soldier?
    (Throw over shoulder and salute)
Do your ears hang low?

ROCKET SHIP

Five, four, three, two, one—BLAST OFF!
    (Children crouch on floor then jump up with
      arms outstretched)
Zoom, zoom, zoom, we're going to the moon.
Zoom, zoom, zoom, we won't be back very soon!
    (Children hold hands and go in circle)
We'll step in and off we'll blast
    (Step into center and raise hands)
In our rocket ship so fast.
    Zoom, zoom, zoom, we're going to the moon.
    (Join hands and circle)
Five, four, three, two, one—BLAST OFF!

SPRING IS ALL ROUND
(Tune: *Old MacDonald Had a Farm*)

Refrain

In the woods, I took a walk
On a sunny day
And as I walked, I looked around
Sure enough I found:

First Verse

Flowers blooming, blooming, blooming
Spring is all around.
    (Fingers bloom from closed fist)

Refrain

Second Verse

Birds a nesting, nesting, nesting
    (Wiggle down into nesting position)
    (Add first verse)

Refrain

Third Verse

Sunny spot so warm, warm, warm
    (Hands together over head to form sun)
    (Add second and first verse)

Refrain

Fourth Verse

Big mud puddle, puddle, puddle
    (Pretend splashing with feet)
    (Add other verses)

Refrain

Fifth Verse

Frogs a croaking, croaking, croaking
    (Squatting position hop)
    (Add other verses)

Recipes for Small Hands

In the childhood memories of every good cook, there's a large kitchen, a warm stove, a simmering pot and a mom.

Barbara Costikyan
"Holiday Entertaining"
New York, *22 Oct. 1984*

A HEALTHY PRESCHOOLER'S DAY is punctuated with nutritious snacks. These "mini-meals" serve as opportunities for exploring new foods and being creative with old favorites. Often, the simple snack he has had a hand in preparing is the one most likely to hit the spot when he's hungry! Fanciful names also go a long way toward helping a child have fun as he is building a taste for and habit of good nutrition.

Cooking provides children with a myriad of learning adventures. Their language skills are expanded as they compare ingredients which look similar, such as sugar and salt, yet are different. They learn new words to describe what is happening—dissolving, grating, shredding, freezing. Math concepts are introduced by counting, sorting and measuring. Motor skills are developed as little hands beat, pour and knead.

Elementary science concepts are experienced as children taste, smell and feel ingredients before and after cooking. They learn about chemical changes as they add yeast to dough and watch bread rise, or add soda and vinegar to gingerbread batter.

Mini-Meal Suggestions

Kabobs—Skewer chunks of fruit, cheese or meat on pretzels. You may include yogurt or cottage cheese for a dip.

Meat cookies—Slices of salami or baloney may be cut in shapes with cookie cutters.

Apple cookies—Core whole apple and slice in circles. Fill core hole or frost apple cookie with peanut butter and raisins.

Fruit sandwich—Slice a banana lengthwise, spread peanut butter between the halves, add raisins, sunflower seeds, etc., if you wish. Can be sliced up for bite size pieces or eaten whole. Or, use slices of apple with cheese or peanut butter between.

Yogurt/fruit pops—Fill popsicle mold, small paper cups or ice cube trays with any mixture of yogurt, fruit juice, crushed fruit. Insert popsicle stick and freeze.

Cheese cartoons—Use cookie cutters to cut special shapes out of cheese. Good for holidays. Cut sandwiches with cookie cutters, too.

Mystery muffins—Fill muffin cups 1/3 full with favorite recipe, then drop in cube of cheese or taste of jam. Cover with batter and bake.

Ants on a log—You or child fill celery with peanut butter and stick raisins along top. Can use cheese, cottage cheese, tuna or egg salad as a filler.

Roll-ups—Slices of beef, ham or turkey, spread with cheese and rolled up. Or add a bit of pineapple or mandarin orange and roll up.

Inside-out sandwich—Start with a slice of bread, wrap with slice of cheese or meat and roll up with bread inside.

Cinnamon toast cutouts—Have kids cut shapes out of bread with cutters. Toast briefly on a cookie sheet under the broiler. Spread with butter and sprinkle with cinnamon sugar.

Peter Rabbit dips—Mix 8 oz. plain yogurt with 1 package dried vegetable soup mix and serve with raw vegetables (celery trees, zucchini, cucumber coins, etc.).

Banana wheels—Let child cut wheels from banana using plastic knife. Roll wheels in dish of wheat germ. Or dip first in yogurt and then roll.

Space balls—Mix together 1 cup honey, 1 cup peanut butter, 2 cups powdered milk. Roll into balls. Eat plain or roll in wheat germ, corn flakes, coconut, nuts, etc.

Cheerio necklace—Have child make edible necklace by threading Cheerios on a string. Use blunt end needle or tightly wrap one end of string with tape to make stiff. (This is great for mothers to make for toddlers before a shopping trip.)

Apple toast—Peel and slice up an apple. Butter slice of bread and place apple slices on top. Sprinkle with cinnamon sugar. Bake on cookie sheet for 15 minutes at 375°.

Slurpies—Whir ice cubes, juice concentrate and water (enough to blend) in blender. Serve in paper cups.

Cheesie popcorn (or cereal)—Mix until coated: 3 cups popped corn with 1/4 cup butter and 1/4 cup grated cheddar cheese. Or mix small Wheat or Corn Chex with above butter and cheese mix.

Surprise lunch—Use cupcake pan for plate. Fill each compartment with one type of food (strawberries, peanuts, cheese cubes, raisins, ham cubes—or whatever you have on hand).

Veggie zoo—Creating a menagerie of vegetable sculpture animals is fun and may even stimulate a new enthusiasm for eating veggies. A few possibilities:

A porcupine with cucumber body and slivered almond quills inserted in little slits on its back, tomato or radish head.

A bear with zucchini body, cherry tomato head, Cheerio eyes and ears (stuck on with soft cream cheese), carrot stick arms and legs.

An elephant with squat zucchini body, short carrot chunk legs, dill pickle trunk, bread-and-butter pickle ears.

(Toothpicks may be used to assemble animals, but parent should supervise eating so children do not put toothpicks in their mouths.)

Fun to Make and Eat

CEREAL SCRAMBLE

3 cups assorted, unsweetened cereal (Cheerios, Wheat Chex, Rice Chex)
1/2 cup pretzel sticks
1/4 cup margarine, melted

Gently mix all ingredients. Spread on baking sheet. Bake at 300° for 30 minutes. Stir occasionally. Store in tightly covered container.

GRANOLA

5 cups oats	1 cup sliced almonds
1 cup sesame seeds	1 cup shredded coconut
1 cup wheat germ	1 cup raisins
1 cup honey	1 cup vegetable oil

Mix dry ingredients. Combine honey and oil and warm in saucepan. Mix well with dry ingredients. Spread out on 2 or 3 baking sheets and bake at 275° for 1 hour or until golden brown. Stir occasionally.

ART SALADS

Sailboat Salad—Wash lettuce leaves, tear and place on plate. Top with peach half, hollow side up. Fill hollow with cottage cheese or mayonnaise topped with nuts. Add toothpick mast stuck through paper sail. (Sail can serve as place card.)

Candle Salad—Wash lettuce. Tear and arrange on plate. Top with pineapple ring. Place banana (cut off ends) in hole of pineapple so it stands like a candle. Add cherry or carrot curl for flame.

1 Cup Salad—Mix 1 cup each: diced bananas, fruit cocktail, tiny marshmallows, crushed pineapple and sour cream. Chill. Serve as salad or dessert.

KIDS' PIZZA

Refrigerator biscuits or English muffin halves

Sauce

6 oz. can tomato paste
1/2 tsp. each oregano, basil

Toppings

Mozzarella cheese, hot dog slices, pineapple, ham, olives, chopped pepper, etc.

Have kids flatten biscuits on cookie sheet (or place muffin halves on sheet). Spread pizza sauce on each and sprinkle with grated cheese. Let each child garnish his pizza as he wishes. Bake at 350° until crust is brown and cheese is bubbly.

CRUNCHY OR SOFT TACOS

This is fun to do with kids because there are so many varied steps which they can do. Have the child shred lettuce, grate cheddar cheese and dice tomatoes (steak knife is just right for child to handle).

Brown hamburger and add package of taco seasoning per directions. (Children may or may not be involved in this stage.)

Buy crispy taco shells or flour tortillas and warm in oven. Add filling to taco or tortilla and let children add their own lettuce, tomato and cheese. (Anticipating kids' reactions will save some grief. Explain, "These are very messy, so don't worry if they fall apart; that's why there's a fork by your plate.")

FANCIFUL BREAD

This dough is not very sticky. It's fun to "play with" as well as being edible when baked. The children will enjoy shaping the dough into teddy bears, turtles, bunnies or other favorite shapes. Currants or nuts may be added for eyes and other features. A favorite rainy day meal might be a pot of vegetable soup or stew accompanied by these personalized little breads.

2 pkgs. dry yeast
2 cups warm water
2 Tbsp. sugar

Place in bowl. *Do not stir*. In 5 minutes add:

2 Tbsp. plus 2 tsp. vegetable oil
2 tsp. salt

Stir in 3 cups flour. Add up to 3 more cups till dough is smooth and elastic. Form dough into ball and place in oiled bowl. Cover with plastic wrap. Let rise 1 hour. Punch and knead a little.

Grease 2 cookie sheets. Shape dough as desired. Brush on glaze of 2 well beaten eggs. Bake at 350° for 45-60 minutes. (Shorter time for smaller shapes.)

JELLO IN THE SNOW

Mix up some Jello. Pour into cupcake tins and place in the snow. Let your child observe how quickly it hardens.

FINGER JELLO

2 envelopes unflavored gelatin
1 (6 oz.) or 2 (3 oz.) pkg. Jello
2 1/2 cups water

Dissolve unflavored gelatin in 1 cup cold water. Set aside. Dissolve Jello in 1 cup boiling water. Add gelatin mixture and 1/2 cup cold water. Pour into lightly greased pan and set in refrigerator until solid (about 2 hours). Cut into squares (or use cookie cutters) and store in airtight container in refrigerator.

Alternative

3 envelopes unflavored gelatin
12 oz. can frozen juice concentrate
12 oz. water

Soften gelatin in thawed juice and bring water to boil. Add juice-gelatin mixture and stir until gelatin is dissolved. (May add extra sweetening.) Follow directions above for chilling.

KICK-THE-CAN ICE CREAM

1 egg	dash of salt
1/4 cup honey	rock salt
1 cup milk	ice
1/2 cup cream	fruit (opt.)
1 tsp. vanilla	

Beat egg and honey. Add rest of ingredients. Fill 2 or 3 lb. coffee can up to 2/3 full with mix (except ice and rock salt). Cover with tight lid. Place in 5 lb. coffee can and pack with ice and rock salt. Cover larger can with lid. Let kids kick the can around the yard or park, or roll it down a hill. Will keep frozen in can about 1 hour if in shade.

TOASTED PUMPKIN SEEDS

2 cups unwashed pumpkin seeds
1 1/2 tsp. Worcestershire sauce
1 1/2 Tbsp. melted butter or margarine
1 1/4 tsp. seasoning salt

After the top has been cut off the Halloween pumpkin, have the child dig out the pumpkin seeds and clean off fairly well, but don't wash. In a bowl, combine seeds, Worcestershire sauce, butter and salt until seeds are coated. Spread on large shallow baking sheet. Bake at 250° for about 1 hour, stirring occasionally until crisp, dry and golden brown.

CUTOUT COOKIES

These cookies allegedly will not stick to cutters and are endorsed by a preschool teacher.

2 1/2 cups flour	1 egg
1 tsp. baking power	1 cup dry oatmeal
1/2 tsp. salt	1 tsp. vanilla
1/4 tsp. nutmeg, cinnamon, allspice	
3/4 cup butter	
1 cup sugar	
2 Tbsp. milk	

Sift flour, baking powder, salt and spices. Add butter, sugar, milk, egg and vanilla and beat. Stir in oats (will be stiff). Roll on floured surface to 1/2 inch thick. Cut shapes and bake at 375° for about 15 minutes.

(For cookie "paint," mix egg yolk and 1/4 tsp. water. Divide into several sections of a muffin tin and mix with a few drops of food coloring. Use small paintbrushes to decorate cookies, then bake.)

AGGRESSION COOKIES

3 cups oatmeal
1 1/2 cups brown sugar
1 1/2 cups flour
1 1/2 cups butter or margarine
1 1/2 tsp. baking powder

Dump all ingredients into large bowl. Mash it! Knead it! Pound it! The longer and harder you mix it, the better it tastes! Roll dough into small balls. Bake on ungreased cookie sheet at 350° for 10-12 minutes.

PAINTBOX COOKIES

(This is a *Sunset* magazine classic.)

These sturdy cookies, baked and glazed ahead, can be painted with food coloring for a rainy day or party project.

2 cups softened butter or margarine
2 cups granulated sugar
2 tsp. vanilla
5 cups flour
5-9 tsp. warm water
1 1/2 lb. powdered sugar
Assorted food colors

Beat butter, granulated sugar and vanilla together. Add flour till thoroughly blended. Roll dough out on ungreased baking sheet to 1/4-3/8 inch thickness. May cut in rectangular shapes, removing excess dough or cut in shapes with floured cutters.

Bake at 300° for 25-30 minutes till dough is pale gold.

Add water to powdered sugar till icing is smooth and thick.

Let cookies cool on pan about 7 minutes, then transfer to foil-covered surface. With back of spoon spread cookies with icing to make smooth surface. Don't cover or disturb till icing is dry to touch (8-24 hours).

Paint with food coloring when dry. May store at room temperature for up to 4 days or freeze for longer storage. Thaw before painting.

To paint "cookie canvases"—use water color brushes and small cups of food coloring undiluted for bright colors or slightly diluted for lighter ones. Food coloring will flow, so allow each color to dry briefly before adding the next.

(These cookies take a bit of advanced planning and baking but are great fun as well as delicious.)

CHAPTER 8

Fun With Science

All the things you want to know
About yourself and how you grow,
About the world in which you live,
What you think, and find and give —
That's Science.

Unknown

YOUNG CHILDREN ARE BORN SCIENTISTS. They have a driving curiosity as they touch, smell, taste, see and hear to learn more about themselves and their world. The basis for understanding scientific concepts begins with a wealth of experiences which a child can repeat over and over again. It is important to allow children the joy of discovery. If children are told all the answers, we are robbing them of this joy and an important learning step.

As parents, you can provide a rich environment of experiences for your child. Be a positive role model by being enthusiastic and help your child develop a process of guessing what might happen, exploring by using all the senses and then discussing what happened. You are opening the door of the world, and your child's mind has been stimulated. Have fun and enjoy these science experiences with your child.

For convenience, science is often subdivided into categories or branches of science. Biology (Living Things), Chemistry (Changes) and Physical Science (Sound and Motion) are the branches of science that this chapter will focus on. Don't let these terms frighten you away. The chapter is structured to allow you and your child to sample each of the major fields of science.

Living Things (Biology)

While exploring the living world, allow your child the opportunity to discover living things with an open mind. Try to disguise any discomfort you may feel toward a particular plant or beastie.

The following sampling of activities involve plants. Learning how plants grow and thrive and experiencing the magic promise of life in a tiny seed will fascinate a child.

Gardens

CARROT GARDEN

Carrots with greens	Water
Shallow bowl	Knife
Pebbles or stone	

Cut off carrot tops about 2 inches down. Take off wilted leaves and place cut end down in a shallow bowl. Place pebbles around carrots to hold them down and fill half full of water. Watch for feathery leaves to grow, beginning in a few days. Keep pebbles moist.

SPONGE GARDEN

Sponge
Small seeds (alfalfa, wheat or leftovers from your
    garden)
Liquid plant food

Sprinkle seeds on a sponge that has been soaked in water and plant food. Place sponge on plate and watch your garden grow! Remember to keep the sponge moist.

LIMA BEANS GARDEN

Lima beans
Construction paper
Paper towel
Glass of water (glass must be clear)

Place the construction paper in the glass so that it touches the edge of the glass (a construction paper tube within the glass). Fill the center of the construction paper tube with moist paper towel. Slip the lima beans between the construction paper and the glass. Keep the paper towel moist. Watch for root and stem growth from the bean seed.

Variation—After growth has begun, turn the glass on its side for a few days to watch how the plant growth responds to the forces of gravity.

SWEET POTATO VINE

Sweet potato
Glass of water

Put the narrow end of a sweet potato into a glass of water. Place in a dark spot and wait for two weeks. Change the water as needed so as to maintain a clean environment for the growing plant. Once the sweet potato has sprouted, place it in a sunny window. This will produce a very pretty vine.

POP BOTTLE GREENHOUSE

2 liter pop bottle
Soil

Seeds, small fern plants, moss, etc.
Water

Cut the bottom off of the pop bottle. Save the top portion. Fill the bottom with soil. Plant the seeds or moss or fern. Moisten the soil. Slit the top portion of the bottle (see diagram) and replace it on the bottom. Place in a warm well lit area. Watch the seeds sprout and the plants grow.

MOLD GARDEN

Pie plate
Water
Foil
Magnifying glass

Several foods (slice of bread, orange peel, leftover rice, cheese, etc.)

On a large pie plate arrange several foods. Sprinkle with water. Cover loosely with foil. (Do not cover airtight.) Place in a cupboard or closet. Check for mold growth in two to three days.

Molds are plants which live in the air but grow rapidly on a host. Study the mold growth with a magnifying glass. Count the types of molds by their shapes and colors.

Variation—Place a slice of bread (made with no preservatives) into a ziplock bag. Place in a cupboard or closet for a few days. Observe any growth. An apple or slice of cheese may substitute for bread.

More Fun With Plants

SHOPPING CART BOTANY

The supermarket is an excellent resource center to obtain materials for exploration and discovery. Consider the following items to explore.

Seeds—Plant a bean, count peas in a pod, discover all the fruits with seeds.

Flowers—Broccoli, artichoke, cauliflower.

Plants without flowers—Mushrooms, dried seaweed (reconstitute).

Stems—Celery.

Roots—Carrots with their green tops, potatoes which are sprouting vines.

MAKE RAISINS

Seedless grapes
Paper towel
Warm, sunny spot

Wash some seedless grapes and put them on a paper plate. Cover with a paper towel to keep them clean. Set the grapes in a sunny, warm spot. In a week or two the grapes will resemble raisins.

A DRINKING CELERY STALK

Celery stalk
Glass of water
Food coloring

Cut the bottom end off two stalks of celery. Put the celery stalks in half a glass of water. Add a few drops of food coloring to the water. After two hours take out one celery stalk. Cut or break the stalk into slices. Note how far the color has risen in the stalk. Leave the other celery stalk in the water for a day. Then cut the stalk in half. Note the distance the color has traveled in the stalk.

Variations—Try daffodils or white carnations in colored water; wait and note any color change. Or place one celery stalk in fresh water and one stalk in salt water; wait a day and note the differences in the two stalks.

Critters

Children have an innate curiosity about the other animals which share their ecosystem (animals, plants and their environment). The following ideas can fulfill some of those natural curiosities.

PETS IN A JAR

Children love collecting. Collecting small wild animals (insects, spiders, worms, moths, caterpillars, etc.) is a favorite with most children. It is important for you to help your child understand that if he takes a living animal from its environment, then it is his responsibility to care for it.

A pet in a jar needs an environment and food that suits it properly. After your child has finished observing the animal or has lost interest in it, it is time to return it to the environment from which it was taken.

A heavy plastic ziplock bag makes a good container for collecting. When you return home, you can transfer the small animal with the environment you collected into a large glass or plastic jar. A lid with holes or an old nylon stocking stretched across the top and secured with a rubber band will allow air circulation for the pet. Or make your own bug zoo.

MILK CARTON BUG ZOO

Quart milk carton
Contact paper
Nylon stocking
Spring clothespin
Cut off peaked top of milk carton. Cut two large

windows on opposite sides of carton. You can cover carton with contact paper if you wish. Put carton in old nylon stocking and trim off stocking about 4 inches above top of carton. Close top of stocking with spring clothespin.

DOWN TO THE POND

You can simply collect a half gallon of pond water and bring it home. The water is full of minute water creatures. You can keep the water for a few weeks without adding anything to it. Look closely for many different kinds of animals. You can also collect sea water.

Tadpoles—In the spring you may be able to

collect frog eggs or tadpoles. Don't take more than 10 eggs. Five to six tadpoles can live in a gallon jar. Be careful not to leave the container in the direct sunlight. Bring home pond water and some pond plants. Tadpoles feed on pond plants or boiled lettuce or spinach. Depending on the kind of tadpole, development will take a month or longer. You will need to return your frog to the pond when it is fully developed. They eat only live insects and need a much larger environment than a gallon jar.

Salamanders—Collect only one or two per jar. They will need fresh pond water and water plants. They feed on small pond animals, but you can use small pieces of cat food or tubiflex worms from the pet store.

DOWN UNDER THE GROUND

Earthworms—Collect half a dozen worms with enough soil to fill half the jar. Also collect some old leaves to go on top of the soil. Keep the jar in a cool part of your house and wrap dark paper around the jar to keep out the light. Unwrap the paper when you want to observe your worms. Sprinkle a few drops of water on top of the soil every few days. You can also add lettuce and other cut-up vegetable scraps to the jar for their food.

Snails and slugs—These make perfect kitchen pets because you can feed them the outside leaves of the lettuce and cabbage you don't use! Add a bit of sand and soil to the bottom of your jar, a bit of moss, and you will have an environment for your slimy friends!

Caterpillars—All a caterpillar does is eat, so it is very important to collect the leaves that you found it eating for food. Caterpillars collected in the spring will finish their cycle in a month or so. Fall caterpillars will not hatch out of their pupa stage until the following spring. Make sure that you add a stick to your jar and that you keep a fresh supply of leaves until they have gone into their pupa stage. Leave a wet cotton ball in the jar. They need the moisture in order to hatch. After your butterfly or moth has hatched, let it go.

For a Grow-a-Butterfly Kit, contact Insect Core Products, P.O. Box 1535, Shaffer, CA 93263; (805) 746-6047.

Bird feeders are excellent places to watch the birds who come to visit. The following are some ideas for homemade bird feeders.

A pinecone which has been rolled in peanut butter
String Cheerios through a piece of yarn
Half of an orange or grapefruit

Cut the two opposite sides from a milk carton,
  place birdseed in the bottom
A pine cone rolled in lard then rolled in birdseed

SHOPPING CART ZOOLOGY

Consider the following items to explore.

Chicken—Investigate skin, muscles, bones
Heart—Beef, sheep, chicken
Bones—Ask your butcher to save large ones
Fish—Find eyes, tongue, teeth, gills

Invertebrates

Squid—Count the arms, find beak, eyes, ink sac
Oysters, Clams, Crab, Shrimp

Eggs-perience

Most animals and plants begin life as an egg cell. A true egg is like a seed. It will contain the embryo and food for the embryo. Mother animals lay eggs so babies will grow inside them. The eggs are full of food that is good for their babies and good for us too. An animal baby needs lots of food in his egg if he must stay in the egg a long time before he hatches. The animal baby needs only a little food if he is going to stay in the egg a short time.

Some eggs stay inside the mother's body while the baby grows, so the eggs don't need much food in them. The growing babies get food from their mother until they are ready to be born.

Bird shells have a hard shell to protect them in case the mother sits down too hard on the nest. Frog eggs and fish eggs are sticky so that they will attach themselves to rocks where they are safer. Some eggs have leathery skins and some have thin sacks. Some animals, like frogs and oysters, lay millions of eggs at one time. Birds think one egg at a time is enough.

In a bird egg, the white part of the egg is called the albumen. The yellow part is the yolk. Both are food for the baby bird. The small, white strings hold the yolk in the center of the egg to protect it. The eggs we buy at the store do not have baby chicks inside of them. The egg farmers hold up their eggs to a strong light and look inside. The eggs with baby chicks inside go back to the mother hen or an incubator until they are ready to hatch.

WHAT CAN YOU DO WITH EGGS?

Float an egg—Eggs usually don't float, but if you pour salt into the water, soon the egg will rise to the surface and float. Fill a glass with hot water (the trick will work faster if the water is hot). Lower an egg (raw or hard boiled) into the water and watch it sink. Now add salt to the water. The salt will make the water cloudy, but wait and watch for the egg to float.

Crack an egg—You can't crush a raw egg with one hand! Hold the egg in the palm of your hand with your fingers wrapped around it. Digging fingernails in is not allowed! The reason the egg won't break is because your cupped hand is similar to the oval shape of the egg. Note: It will break if you squeeze it end to end.

Soak an egg—Put a raw egg in a glass full of vinegar. Leave it there for a couple of days. Touch carefully and you will feel a rubber egg! The vinegar (acid) will dissolve the shell leaving the raw egg inside the thin rubbery membrane under the shell.

Silver egg—Turn a hard-boiled egg into a silver egg. Light a candle and hold egg over it with a wire loop or tongs. Turn it until the egg is covered with soot. Gently drop the egg into a glass of water, and it will appear to turn silver.

Color eggs—With condensed milk—Place a small amount of condensed milk into several containers. Add a couple of drops of different food coloring into each container. Paint with a small paintbrush. Colors will be bright and glossy. The colors may run together, but this adds to the unique effect. *The eggs will be tacky for about four days.*

Color eggs—With tissue paper—Tear or cut small pieces of colored tissue paper. Lay one at a time on the egg which had been moistened with water. As the paper adheres to the egg, it also transfers some of its dye. After the egg is covered with the paper and it has dried, remove the paper from the egg.

(See *Treasury of Basic Craft Recipes* for egg dye recipe.)

Look for eggs—On leaves, branches, under stones and in the dirt you may find insect eggs, snail and slug eggs. In ponds you may find frog eggs and fish eggs. Watch a bird nesting. Look for spider egg sacks around windows and under eaves. Have an egg hunt with real eggs, plastic eggs, paper eggs, etc.

Cook and eat an egg—We use eggs in many ways for cooking. Try eggnog, scrambled eggs, hard- and soft-boiled eggs, meringue (baked on graham crackers), eggs in pancakes or for custard.

PUT IT TOGETHER AND SEE WHAT HAPPENS

INGREDIENT	MIX WITH
Water	Any liquid or powder
White vinegar (you can extend with 1/2 water, 1/2 vinegar)	Baking soda
	Volcano mixture: In a small container add 1 tsp. of soda. Then drop vinegar (you can add red food color for effect) onto the soda.
	Shine a penny: Give child a small dish of salt and a small dish of vinegar and some dirty pennies. Rub pennies with the salt and vinegar with a cotton swab.
Salad oil (vocabulary--insoluble)	Colored water in a plastic pop bottle. Screw on lid and then shake the bottle. What happens?
Food colors (dilute with water to extend)	Add to water to make different colors. With younger children use one color to begin with.
	Rainbow magic: In a shallow cake or pie pan put in 1/2 cup of milk. Add drops of food color and drips of dish detergent on the side of the pan. Watch the colors explode!
Flavoring extracts	Mix with water for "perfumes"--mint, strawberry, orange, etc.
Cornstarch (call it goop, add green food coloring and call it "Oobleck" from Dr. Seuss	Mix with water to a paste consistency and then squeeze (use a tray to catch). Leave overnight and observe the change. Add water again.
Flour, sugar, sugar cubes, salt, baby powder, powdered milk	Use these powders to mix with any of the liquids. The results will be color changes, bubbles, smells, surprises and a mess!

INGREDIENT	MIX WITH
Ivory soap	Mix with water and beat with eggbeater
Unflavored gelatin	Mix with water and ice--what happens? What happens if you heat the mixture? You can repeat the process over and over. Don't forget to make jello to eat!
Mud--from ground or use potter's clay	Add water (outside activity!)
Sand	Explore wet and dry (outside)
Ice	Mix with water
Cornmeal, sand, pea gravel, beans, rice,	Wonderful for sorting, measuring, pouring-- in a tub with high sides

Changes (Chemistry)

You can provide your child with a variety of solutions, powders and sensory materials so that he can experience the process of chemistry—combining, separating, absorbing, heating (with parental help) and cooling. Encourage your child to measure using various sizes of containers, weighing using a simple balance scale, pour, mix and filter. Listed below are a few activities to get you and your child started. Remember too that cooking is chemistry!

Always remind your child that solutions and powders are not for tasting—only if parent directed. Mix in ice cube trays or plastic egg cartons. Do mixing on a tray to minimize mess.

More Experiments

CRYSTAL GARDEN

2 Tbsp. salt
2 Tbsp. water
1 Tbsp. ammonia
2 Tbsp. bluing (in soap section of grocery store)
1 glass bowl or empty tuna fish can
1 charcoal briquette

Place the charcoal in the container and then help your child pour the first four ingredients over the charcoal. Add drops of food coloring, then leave undisturbed for a day or so and watch it grow.

DANCING RAISINS AND SPAGHETTI

1 Tbsp. raisins
Uncooked spaghetti (2 or 3 pieces)
1 jar
2 cups water
1 Tbsp. baking soda
3 Tbsp. vinegar

Add baking soda to the jar of water. Stir until it dissolves. Break uncooked spaghetti into 1-inch pieces and put them and the raisins into the solution. Stir in the vinegar. Wait and watch!

HIDDEN COLORS
(Paper chromatography)

Coffee filter paper
Scissors

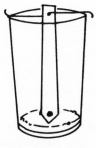

Water soluble black ink (felt pens, etc.)
Water and a clear glass
Paper clip

Cut the filter paper into strips with a pointed end. Make a small dot of concentrated ink 1/2 inch from the pointed bottom (the drop of ink becomes more concentrated the longer the pen sets on the spot). Open the paper clip and hang the filter paper from the clip (see diagram). Put just enough water in the bottom of the glass for the filter tip to touch. Wait and observe. Pull the filter paper out when the water has risen to the top of the paper.

VINEGAR ROCKET LAUNCHER

Cork
Paper streamers
Quart soda bottle
Paper towel
1/2 cup vinegar
1 tsp. baking soda
1/2 cup water

To make "rocket," attach streamers to top of cork. Put water and vinegar into soda bottle. Put the baking soda on a 4 in. by 4 in. paper towel, roll and twist ends to keep soda inside. Outside house, drop the paper into the bottle and put cork on as tightly as you can. Stand back and wait. Carbon dioxide gas forms and pressure builds up inside the bottle causing the cork to POP!

(See *Recipes for Small Hands* for *Kick the Can Ice Cream* for an edible experiment with "changes.")

Sounds and Motion (Physics)

Your child plays with physics every day. It is not important for him or her to understand why things happen as much as it is for him to observe, to test and to make a prediction about what might happen.

MOTION

You can follow the track a moving object makes.

Marble run—Dip marbles in paint and roll them inside a pie pan or box lid. You can lay paper inside the container if you want to save the track.

Lazy susan art—Put a sheet of paper on a lazy susan, turn and make a mark with a felt tip pen. You can try this on a record player turntable, too.

Marble raceway—Make a marble raceway from toilet paper tubes, paper towel tubes, etc. Use lots of tape to hold the raceway together; elevate one end, then send the marbles or small balls down the chute.

Ramps—Use any kind of a ramp to give your

child experience with motion. Blocks provide a wonderful experience for children to explore physical concepts.

Frisbee—Staple two paper plates together to make a homemade frisbee and send it spinning.

Water play—In a plastic tub of water or the kitchen sink, use plastic tubing, basters, eggbeaters, straws to blow items across the water, objects to sink and float. Put a hole in a plastic pop bottle with an ice pick. Fill the bottle with water and screw on the lid. Squeeze the bottle and see what happens.

SOUNDS

Glassical sounds—Add various amounts of water to glass jars or drinking glasses and use a pencil as a striker. What gives a high note? What gives a low note? Are some sounds quiet? Loud? Try making up a tune.

Shakers—Use beans, rice, gravel, marbles, etc., inside various containers with lids. Listen for the different sounds. You can make a sound-matching game by using film containers and filling two of each item.

Pluckers—Place rubber bands around a sturdy box or hammer nails into a board and stretch rubber bands from nail to nail and then pluck and listen for different sounds. Different sizes of rubber bands may give you different sounds.

Tin can telephone—Make a hole in the end of each tin can and then push end of string through and tie to match stick. Stretch out the line and talk and listen.

Speaking tube—Take an old piece of garden hose and add a funnel to each end. Stretch out and find a friend to talk and listen with!

MACHINERY

Save that old alarm clock or other broken machine. Cut off the cord if it is electrical and give your child a few small screwdrivers. Children love to take things apart! Garage sales and secondhand stores are also good resources for machines.

MAGNETISM

In addition to just finding out what your child can attract with a magnet, try these magnetic games:

Fishing—You will need a small stick with a string tied on the end and a magnet attached to the string. Attach paper clips to paper fish and try catching the fish with your magnetic fishing pole.

Magnetic puppet show—Attach metal tack or washer to a small toy or a paper figure. Use a shoe box for a stage. Hold magnet under the side of the shoe box and put the toy figure on top. Move the magnet and watch the moving object on the top of the box.

LIGHT AND SHADOWS

A flashlight with batteries to spare is a good beginning. You can add colored cellophane to extend experimenting. If you shine a red light on a boldly colored picture, what happens to some of the colors? Try another color on the flashlight.

Dark box—You need a box large enough for your child's head to be inside. Drape a dark cloth over the opening. Paint the box black (inside) and attach the dark cloth to the top of one side. Your child then can put the box on a table and look in it with a flashlight. Have a variety of shiny objects—combs, tubes, glow-in-the-dark stickers—available to look at.

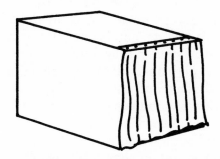

Mirrors—Acrylic mirrors or heavy pieces of mylar glued on cardboard are safest to use. Look at the sky, look behind you, look over walls, look around corners. Hang a mirror ball up in a sunny window. You can find these at party/decoration shops—or make your own!

Tape two small mirrors together at right angles and then place objects in front of mirrors.

You can make a kaleidoscope by taping three

mirrors together in a triangle and then placing objects in the center.

Mirror tricks—Place a mirror next to pictures of symmetrical objects or half of an object. What happens? Can you make the pictures whole? Can you make the picture disappear? What else happens?

Shadows—Inside use a lamp shining on a blank wall. A slide projector gives the clearest image for shadows, but lamps work fine. Your child can make shadows with his/her hands or make simple stick puppets and have a shadow puppet show. Outside on a sunny day, play shadow tag by trying to step on someone's shadow and then he is "It."

What kind of shadows can you make? Does your shadow ever change? Can you hide your shadow? Draw around your shadow with a piece of chalk. Can your shadow stand on someone's head?

FLYING THINGS

See *Arts and Crafts* for directions for making a paper airplane, parachute and paper bag kite. Below are directions for two additional easy-to-make and fly kites.

Sled kite—Open up a paper bag (cut bottom out) and attach string to each small side. A small child can simply use a 6 ft. to 10 ft. piece of string, and the center becomes the handle.

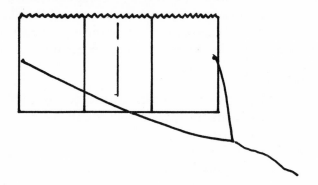

Plastic bag kite—Simply take a plastic bag with handles and attach a string to the two handles and let 'er fly.

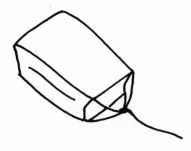

BUBBLES

A soap bubble is one of the thinnest things that can be seen without a microscope. A soap bubble is 5,000 times thinner than a hair from your head! Blowing bubbles can be fun; it also can be hard, stimulating work. Many scientists and architects work with bubbles—there's lots to see and learn.

RECIPE FOR SUPER BUBBLES

1 qt. warm water
2/3 cup liquid dishwashing soap (Dawn® works well)

1/3 cup glycerine (from drugstore)

Mix in dishpan and use immediately. Six-pack holders, jar rings, funnels, plastic hangers all make good bubblers. (See *Treasury of Basic Craft Recipes* for more ideas and directions for making a *Giant Bubble Maker*.)

Equipping Your Lab

Your child's most useful tools are his/her senses. The following are additional items you may wish to provide.

Magnifying glass
Eyedroppers
Small tasting spoons from an ice cream shop
Ice cube trays, clear plastic cups and plastic egg
    cartons for mixing and collecting
Bug box
Tweezers
Plastic tray with sides to contain spills
Gallon plastic jars or glass for pet environments
Flashlight

To buy from the grocery, drug and/or hardware store

Baking soda, for volcanoes
Vinegar, to shine pennies

Birdseed, to plant, use in collage
Popcorn, to pop, use in collage
Indian corn, to place in a dish of water and watch
  it grow
Beans
Steel wool, to use with magnets
Straws
Ziploc® bags
Salad oil, for mixing with water, rubbing on
  brown paper
Soap (Dawn® or Joy®), for bubbles
Food extracts
Chicken wings
Whole fish, to make fish prints
Hearts to examine
Epson salts, to waterpaint, sprinkle with salt and
  watch what happens
Magnets
Balloons
Corks
Candles
Paper clips (steel), for magnet work
Wax
Sponges

To buy from pet store

Crickets

Goldfish, water snails
Guppies
African water frogs and pocket mice—make low-
  care pets and cause no allergies

To buy from garage sales

Old clocks, machines, fur scraps and other
  discards

To collect for free

Pond water
Tadpoles—remember to return them to their
  home
Worms—keep moist at all times and return to
  garden
Spiders—return to garden
Sow bugs
Leaves, weeds, flowers
Seeds of all kinds
Abandoned bird nests
Rocks
Humus—wonderful to search through for snails
  and other insects that live underground
Molds—check your refrigerator
Rotten logs—take apart for lots of surprises
Bone
Feathers
Shells

Adventures Away From Home

Up into the cherry tree
Who shall climb but little me?
I held the trunk with both my hands
And looked abroad on foreign lands.

Robert Louis Stevenson

ENJOY THESE YEARS by treating yourself and your preschooler to a variety of outings. Short excursions, traveling (by car and airplane), eating out and camping are all activities that families can enjoy with young children. Prior planning is always important, and this chapter offers helpful suggestions. For happy adventuring it's best to: Keep it Simple, Special, Flexible and Safe!

KEEP IT SIMPLE

Try mini-outings—Take 30 minutes to go to the park. You'll find even short stints refresh you and your child.

Take the bare essentials—Kids are champs at turning sticks, puddles and pebbles into captivating play things.

BE FLEXIBLE

Enjoy the impromptu—Relax with your toddler's idea of fun, even if it's picking dandelions rather than watching the bears at the zoo.

Try again—Even if everything goes wrong, don't get discouraged. The effort to try again will be rewarded with a string of happy memories of outings.

Water means wet—Always carry a towel and a change of clothes. No matter the season or your rules, expect your child to want to wade and splash near water.

Be ready for unknowns—Keep boxed juices, a box of crackers, pens and paper handy. They'll be appreciated when traffic or fun extends your schedule.

MAKE IT SPECIAL

Let the children choose—Discuss trips with your preschooler. Offer him a choice of two or three possibilities or have him list his favorites and pick one destination each week.

Enjoy yourself—Invite another Mom along. You'll be interested in staying longer if you have an adult along for conversation .Also, problem solving on excursions may be easier with another adult along.

PLAY IT SAFE

Always buckle up—Remember, it's the law! Children may get restless in their car seats on long trips, so take breaks to exercise muscles or have an adult sit next to him to amuse him (see *Travel Tips* in this section). Be sure to secure items inside the car, stowing them out of the way, or better yet, in the trunk. Serious injuries result from objects flying around inside the car in an accident.

Keep a first aid kit handy—Equip it with soap, bandages, insect sting relief, sterile pads, tape and children's pain reliever. (See *Camping* section for additional first aid kit ideas.)

Places to Go and Things to See

Every city/town has major attractions and special places to visit. Look for museums, arboretums, water slide parks, zoos, wildlife reserves, aquariums, swimming pools and beaches, libraries (story hours), planetariums, observatories, city hall or state capital buildings, waterfalls, parks, local industries and churches. Get listings and maps of local parks and visit a different one each week. Call ahead for possible special programs and to make reservations, if needed, for all outings.

Everyday errands can be short, fun excursions for preschoolers. A trip to the post office can mean buying a stamp and mailing a letter or artwork to a friend, relative or to himself! Have your child watch the butcher at the grocery store or peek in at the drycleaners. Stop at the dime store for him to select something and buy it. Check out the craft store and let him purchase some materials for a project later.

Here is a list of ideas to get you started thinking about places and activities your preschooler may find exciting:

Walk, walk, walk—At different times of the year, in the rain or snow, around the neighborhood, in a shopping mall, through a college campus, to a local park or school playground.

Organized "Volksmarches," family-oriented "peoples walks" are available free. Contact the American Volkssport Association National Office, Suite 203, Phoenix Square, 1001 Pat Brooker Road, Universal City, TX 78148 for information on local Volkssport chapters and walks.

Combine walks with picnics, scavenger or treasure hunts to look for craft supplies, find recyclables to turn in for cash, etc.

Picnic anywhere and often. How about a breakfast picnic or a car picnic? At a shopping mall, in a park, in a nearby town? Combine picnics with many excursions.

Water—Visit a beach, lake, river, pond. Feed the ducks, wade, dig for clams, collect rocks, shells, feathers. Make a collage when you get home. Water means wet. *Expect* your child to want to wade (swim) and splash, no matter the season. Take extra clothing. Always carry a towel in the car.

Transportation oriented—Take a boat, train, bus, subway, trolley ride to a nearby town. Tour piers, loading docks, ports. Visit the airport, train station or a boat marina. Find a museum on planes, trains or boats and perhaps a restaurant with a transportation theme for lunch.

Animals and fish—Visit a farm, dairy, a fish hatchery, go fishing. Go to a pet store and purchase a pet fish, turtle, etc. Find a pony ride. Visit your local Humane Society or animal protection agency. Go to a state or county fair.

Plants—Visit a plant nursery, pick out a plant to buy and care for. Go to a U-pick garden or orchard for fresh fruits and vegetables.

Bicycle riding—Child seats are available to attach to bicycles. Don't forget approved safety helmets for everyone—look for the ANSI or Snell Memorial Foundation sticker.

Sports—Try roller skating, ice skating, bowling. Call for special times or programs for young children. Go swimming often, finding indoor pools during inclement weather.

Mountains—Go to the mountains different times of the year. Play in the snow, go sledding, innertubing, sliding, skiing, build a snowman. See the changing leaves. Find a glacier-fed stream.

Senior citizens—Visit an elderly neighbor or a local retirement center. "Adopt" a grandmother/ grandfather.

Fire and police departments—Check to see whether a visit can be arranged.

Local industries—Toy maker, confectioner, garment maker, ice cream factory, bakery, furniture maker, dairy, cannery, bottler, etc.

Ethnic stores and communities—Experience new music, foods, costumes, toys, traditions, religions, festivals, language, toys and special events.

Construction sites—Lots of things to see and talk about. Create stories and do some pretending.

Car wash—Call to find out the best times to come and to see if you can ride through as the car is washed.

Thrift shop—Pick up fun clothes for dress-up trunk or let your child spend his allowance money. Great bargains!

Special events—Watch for newspaper listings of parades, the circus, rodeos, children's theater shows, puppet shows or live performances, state or county fairs and special exhibits. Purchase tickets and mark the dates on your calendar so you don't forget to attend! Contact your Chamber of Commerce and State Department of Tourism for listings of things to do in your area.

Nature Walks

Nature walks are for sharing, talking, meeting people and growing in many ways. Walks are times to learn about the environment and our place within that environment.

While on a nature walk take time to stop and use your senses. Look for different plants and animals and listen for sounds of animals. Touch living and non-living components of the ecosystem (animals, plants and their environment). Smell the fresh air and the plants in nature and possibly taste some wild berries. (Caution: Be aware of poisonous plants before touching or tasting.)

A nature walk can be around the neighborhood or in the local park. You may like to make a list of items to look for or collect. Often, however, it is better to first just go out to explore, using your senses as your tools and your open mind to experience the world.

COLLECTIONS

You may decide to collect some items to bring home for further observation or perhaps to make a collage. Keep in mind that living things are best left in their homes for others to enjoy. Never take an entire plant or pluck it up by its roots.

The following is a list of suggested ecosystems to explore and a few ideas to get you started in your discoveries. Don't offer too much direction. Let your child be the observer.

OBSERVATIONS

Under or beside a rock or log (return it to its original position when observations are finished). You may find slugs, snails, toads, insects, worms, moss. Smell the moisture, feel the various textures.

On a sidewalk—Look for footprints (who has been there?), wet leaves, ants, grass in cracks, puddles to splash in.

On, in or under a tree or bush—Look for nuts and fruit to possibly taste (know your plants before doing this). Look for birds, insects and other small animals to watch and listen to. Observe flowers, pinecones, bark, branches, sap, nests, toadstools.

In or near a pond or lake—Look for cattails, water lilies, ducks, fish, your own reflection, insects, leaves, seeds, algae, moss, frogs, tadpoles, turtles, mud, rocks, stones and animal prints.

At the beach—Listen, watch and feel as you experience sand, seagulls, waves and water. Examine seashells (these are homes for some animals), driftwood, seaweed, insects, crabs, clams. Where is the tide?

In a pile of dirt—Look for insects, seeds, worms, rocks, pebbles. Note the colors and textures of soil, gravel, sand. Run your fingers and bare toes through the dirt.

In a garden or on a lawn—Look for dandelions and other seeds, four-leaf clovers, birds, bunnies, squirrels, flowers, grasses, feathers, vegetables, slugs.

Types of Walks

Some suggested types of nature walks might include:

Weather walks—In the rain or snow or on a windy day.

Night hikes—Listen to the night sounds. Look for owls, raccoons, etc. Look for patterns of the stars and note the shape of the moon. A flashlight covered with red cellophane (animals cannot detect red light) is fun to take along.

A pond watch—Bring a clear plastic bottle and collect a specimen to bring home and watch what grows.

A scavenger hunt—Give your child a paper bag with pictures of various objects he might find in a particular ecosystem. Send the child out to find those items pictured.

A leaf gathering—This walk is often most fun in the fall when the colors are changing. Go to the library to find a book which explains why leaves change colors. Collect leaves and paste them to construction paper. Identify them and string together to make a leaf book. Look at the veins in the leaf. Talk about the veins in the leaf and your own veins. Note the similarities. Sort the leaves into categories by size, shape or deciduous vs. coniferous.

My dishes went unwashed today,
I didn't make the bed,
I took his hand and followed
Where his eager footsteps led.

Oh yes, we went adventuring,
My little son and I—
Exploring all the great outdoors
Beneath the summer sky.

We wandered in a crystal stream
We wandered through a wood—
My kitchen wasn't swept today,
But life was gay and good.

Author unknown

Nature Crafts

PRESSED LEAF COLLAGE

Collection of leaves
Old crayons
2 sheets waxed paper
Iron (adult should handle this)
Plastic knife or crayon sharpener
Glitter (optional)

Arrange your collection of leaves on sheet of waxed paper. Scrape crayon shavings onto paper so they fall onto leaves. If desired, sprinkle glitter on leaves also. Cover collage with other sheet of waxed paper. Have an adult iron over this collage with medium iron. A construction paper frame can be cut to serve as a mat for this collage. This is lovely to hang in a window where the sun can filter through.

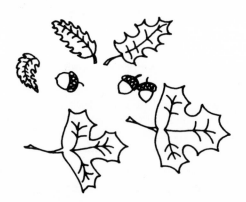

LEAF OR BARK RUBBINGS

Collected leaves and pieces of bark
Peeled crayons
Drawing paper

Arrange leaves and bark under sheet of paper. Hold paper firm (perhaps use masking tape to fasten to table). Rub crayon on its side over the nature items. The veins and outline of the leaves and texture of the bark will "appear" through the paper.

DRIED FLOWERS

Summer or autumn flowers
String
Hanger

Cut a bouquet of flowers or interesting weeds. (Often delicate flowers such as baby's breath or Queen Anne's lace are good for this). Tie the bouquet and hang it upside down (a hanger is good for this) in a dark, dry place such as a closet or attic for two weeks. Some of the flowers will dry better than others. These are lovely arranged in a vase or used to trim a gift.

Variation—Flowers can also be dried in clean dry sand or a mixture of equal parts cornmeal and borax. Put a 1-inch layer of sand or the cornmeal/borax mixture in the bottom of a shoebox. (Adult help with this.) Gently place flower upside down on top of this, then cover with another layer of the same. Put the top on the box and set in a cool dry place for 10 days (sand) to three weeks (cornmeal mixture). Gently remove flowers and brush off drying medium with paintbrush. (Some flowers are better for this than others.)

PRESSED FLOWERS

Fresh flowers
Paper towels or tissue paper
Newspapers
Stack of heavy books

Pick flowers first thing in the morning and gently dry off any dew on the petals. Place flowers between paper towels or tissue paper. Put a pile of newspaper under and on top, then add a large stack of books. After two weeks the flowers will be ready to use. These can be glued on a piece of burlap or felt for bookmarks or on a plain piece of paper for stationery.

SHELL ART

Variety of seashells   Terra cotta pot
Small boxes   Glue

If your trip to the seashore includes collecting shells, it's fun to display them at home as a reminder of the trip. First, be sure the shells are clean and no sand or little animals are still inside. Soaking the shells in a mild solution of laundry bleach and water, then allowing them to dry in the sun is a good way to do this. (Adult help with this.) If necessary, use a nut pick or tweezers to remove anything remaining in the shell.

Select items to decorate and glue the shells in place. A small box becomes a jewelry box, the outside of the meat tray can be decorated as a frame (cut a space in the center to place a photo or child's artwork). A plain pot can be dressed up with shells glued to the outside, etc.

NATURE COLLAGE

Items gathered in woods—leaves, nuts, pebbles, twigs, bark, etc.
Glue
Styrofoam tray or sturdy box top
Paint or construction paper

Paint or cover background of tray or box with paper. Arrange nature collection in random design or create a forest scene. (Shells, seaweed and small pieces of driftwood and sand could create a seascape.) Glue in place.

Travel Tips—Car

"Blankie"—The first thing to pack is the favorite blanket or cuddly toy!

Ball—Take rest breaks often. Play with a big ball (an inflatable beach ball packs well), frisbee, balloon or run races to exercise cramped muscles.

Stow gear in lots of zippered bags but expect the car to get messy. Avoid taking toys with lots of small parts.

Snacks—Take along snack foods and fresh fruits. Boxed drinks with straws attached are great. Try a thermos of water if spillage is a problem. Refillable

squeeze bottles with "spout" like the athletes use are good for little ones (who won't squirt each other).

Disposable wipes or washcloth in plastic bag washed out at rest stops is a must. Consider a towel for emergency spills (it can also be used in the window to shade sun).

Pillow—Pack a small pillow for each child. These can also be used as lap pads for coloring projects. Pillows worn like a collar are now available for infants, too.

Overnight—If stopping overnight:

A. Pack one small bag with everything the family needs to take into the motel. Unpacking and re-packing the car won't be necessary.

B. Try to find a motel with an indoor pool (pack swimming suits!) or a play area. Wear everyone out!

Maps—For older children, give them their own packet of maps and brochures. They will have fun pretending to plot the route and talk about what they will or did see on their trip. Combine with trip diary idea (see *Games* below).

Toys and drawing materials—For young toddlers and infants, tie toys onto the car seat with a shoelace or cord—they can "find" their toys when dropped.

For older children, loosely pack a knapsack or bag

of special toys for each child. Parents can have a "goodie" bag of surprises which they can reach into and give something to each child periodically during the trip to add to their bag. A new toy will hold attention for a long time while it is being discovered. Keep toys "new" by playing with them only on car trips. Add to your collection of trip toys whenever you see some special item.

Suggested toys

Magic slates, small people, cars, wiggly animals, soft picture books, puppets, magnetic games, "pocket" games, travel games, mail catalogs and brochures.

Drawing materials

Clipboard with crayon or pencil attached, fancy pens or pencils, washable marking pens, stickers, tape, rainbow crayon.

Music—If your car doesn't have a tape player, take a portable one. Lots of children's music tapes are available at your toy or bookstore. If tastes in music differ, consider separate tape players and earphones. Sing-a-longs and fingerplays are fun. (See *Fingerplay* section.) Storybooks with cassette tapes are great. Record some of your children's favorite stories on a cassette for them to listen to while looking at the book. Make up silly songs about your trip using familiar tunes. or put silly words to old favorites,

"Row, row, row your squash . . ."

Games

A. Trip diary—Make a "book" for each child before going on the trip with cardboard and paper, stapled or bound with yarn. Bring a gluestick. Have the children make a trip diary—draw a picture on the cover, cut out pictures from brochures along the way, make a map and draw the route, glue in postcards, add photographs.

B. "Official Spotter"—Ask a child to report when he sees a plane, bird, boat, certain sign, etc.

C. Play "I see something that is (a color.) Child tries to guess.

D. Hand puppets are fun. (See *Arts and Crafts* for easy-to-make puppets.)

E. Travel Bingo—Make a game before you leave. Draw or cut from a magazine pictures of what you expect to see on your trip—bus, tow truck, stop sign, cow, horse, etc. Put six or eight of these pictures on a page and let your child cross them out as he sees them. For a more permanent game paste your pictures to cardboard and cover with clear contact paper. Crayon markings will wipe off.

This book—Take along this book as a resource of projects and games for entertainment during your trip and when you reach your destination!

Travel Tips—Airplane

PRE-PLANNING

Nap time—Plan your flight to coincide with nap time, if possible.

Tickets—Pick up tickets in advance. Call early to get seat assignments and request the bulkhead (more room).

Call ahead—Check with the airlines ahead of time for regulations on car seats (check in baggage or carry baby on board?), carry-on luggage, stowing strollers.

Pediatrician—Check with your pediatrician for

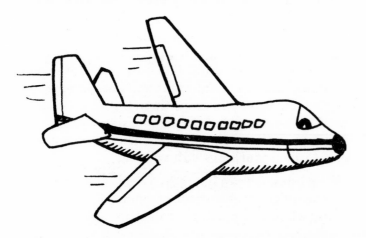

ideas on travel, especially if your child is prone to colds, ear problems or motion sickness.

Ground transportation—Reserve ground transportation ahead of time. Find a rent-a-car agency that will rent child car seats and be sure to reserve one.

Label all luggage—Put identification on all luggage, including carry-ons before you leave home.

IDEAS FOR CARRY-ON ITEMS

Stroller—A collapsible "umbrella-type" is useful for quick connections and tired little feet. Consider a harness or wrist attachment for young walkers.

Snacks—Bring crackers, juice, small boxes of raisins, cheese chunks, etc. Children do not understand flight delays or holding patterns. Chewing gum or lollipops should be given on take-offs and landings to help clear the ears. Infants and toddlers should suck on pacifiers or bottles. If your baby is crying during descent and refuses to take a bottle, try dipping your finger in sugar and let him suck on that.

Clothing—Dress your child for comfort. Especially on longer flights, if you want Aunt Bessie to see him in his Sunday best, have your child change clothes right before landing. Keep a sweater handy also. Cabin temperatures at cruising altitudes are generally cooler.

Expect the unexpected—Pack medications, formula, baby food, diapers, handiwipes and additional clothing to cover delays, cancelled flights and lost luggage. Bring a portable changing pad and plastic bags for soiled diapers. Please be considerate of others in disposing of diapers!

Toys—Good choices are favorite books, a cuddly animal or blanket, tape player and cassettes and something *new*! Give older children their own knapsack to carry on board filled with their things.

DAY OF FLIGHT

Time—Allow enough time for you to arrive at the airport, park, check in, find and reach the gate, and board the plane, with your sanity still intact!

Eating Out With Preschoolers

Dining out with children makes special demands on a restaurant: fast service, booster seats/highchairs, child-sized portions, and a friendly and tolerant staff. When looking for a family restaurant, call ahead and don't be afraid to ask whether or not children are welcome. It helps to remember that the best of planning is not foolproof. Every parent has had their

child fall apart just as the entree is being served. A contingency plan is always needed, such as eating in shifts or taking the rest of your meal home in a "doggie" bag. Your nerves will be saved, and the restaurant will appreciate your consideration of their other guests. The following suggestions should help make your meal as enjoyable as possible. Bon Appetit!

BEFORE YOU GO

Time of day—You are best off if you choose to dine out at an early hour. If you keep to your child's schedule, he will be hungry and more cooperative. Also, dining when the restaurant is less crowded allows them to cater to your special requests.

Reservations—Make them! This is when you find out how "child friendly" the restaurant is. Depending on your own situation, reserve a booth, corner table (great for coloring or quietly playing on the floor), or a window table (this one is good with older children too).

Pack right

A. Bring a bib and baby wipes. Don't expect the restaurant to have either.

B. Often the "seat belts" are missing or broken in highchairs at restaurants. Bring a man's tie, a dishtowel or the brightly colored link toys along to hold baby into chair.

C. Create a "busy bag" and keep it in the car. This can be a few quiet toys, coloring books, crayons, etc. Check through the *Games and Imaginary Play* section of this book for ideas to amuse your child while waiting.

D. Crackers, raisins, a few grapes will keep your child happy until his food arrives.

MEAL TIME

Order ahead—Some restaurants may take the order over the phone and have it ready when you get there (pizza).

Familiar food—Order what your child likes.

Eating out is not the best time to experiment with new foods.

Waiting—Ice cubes and straws are fascinating to little ones. It may be necessary to have one person order while the other takes your toddler for a walk outside.

Dessert—As soon as your child grows restless, order his dessert. A dish of ice cream, though messy, usually will keep him happy while you finish your meal.

Conversation—A second cup of coffee is probably unrealistic, so don't expect it!

Camping

Camping is for fun! Children love playing, eating and sleeping outdoors. Tense moments may arise, but you are there to enjoy one another—even when the draining noodles fall into pine needles, someone forgot to pack the salt, and the children fall into the creek in their last set of dry clothes.

How one handles the unexpected and improvises in a semi-wilderness teaches important values and builds respect, understanding and family closeness. Although camping develops appreciation for the comforts of civilization usually taken for granted, it also brings the rewarding realization that man can live happily without these conveniences, an astounding experience for many children.

Camping trips are taken for many different reasons—so Dad can go fishing, to see a new part of the country inexpensively, for fun with friends or, best of all, to live simply, close to one another and nature.

Here are some helpful tips to keep in mind to help make your camping trip a more enjoyable experience for all:

Camping chores—Foster cooperation. Commensurate with the age of the child, have your youngster help unload the car, sort stakes and tent poles, unroll sleeping bags, gather wood, etc.

Tolerate dirt—If your children are warm and relatively dry, they will be happy with the simple existence and lack of fuss.

Double up—Camp with another family. You can share the responsibilities, babysitting, disasters and laughs. Couples can even take turns getting away for a day of fishing and/or overnight backpack.

Take ten—Leave time for exploring and collecting, building a driftwood castle at the shore, looking for birds' nests, watching a bug, looking for elves and leprechauns, etc.

ADVANCED PLANNING

Reservations—These are essential. Call your campsite ahead of time. Most national and state parks and some private campsites take reservations. Write the Forest Service, U.S. Department of Agriculture, 14th and Independence Ave., S.W., Washington, DC 20250 for the *National Forest Maps and Campground Directory*. Look in your telephone book for listings of U.S. Forest Service Regional Offices for local camping areas. National and State Park Department maps and directories are available from the National Park Service in Washington, DC and from state capitals. Contact your local State Park Service also.

Gear list—Use the list in this section as a guideline. Check with camping friends for other ideas. Some camping equipment stores have lists of gear they suggest. Try borrowing or renting equipment until familiar with needs and desires of your family. Even if you expect to do car-camping only, carefully study backpacking equipment, as it is lighter, warmer, more compact and usually versatile enough. A larger tent and stove, ice chest and lantern would probably be the main additions for family-car-camping. Plan for inclement, cold, hot and dry weather no matter what the season.

Tyke gear

Pack favorite animal or blanket
A walker, it can double as a highchair
Portable potty chair
Baby back carrier for day hikes
Small folding camp table

Expectations—As long as everyone agrees on or understands what others want out of the trip before going, tensions may be reduced. Do you want to teach, relax, have the children play while adults work, take the family pet, stay clean the last day for a visit on the way home, etc.? This is especially important if another family is along.

Trial run—You might want to check out your equipment and system with a trial run. Pitch the tent in the back yard and try to resist going in and out of the house for items you might have forgotten. Keep a running list. You might also plan to try an outdoor dinner at the park with your camping stove. Check out what utensils you need and be sure the stove works this year!

PLANNING FOR SAFETY

First aid kit—This can be a ziplock-type bag or a child's lunch box painted white with a red cross on it. Stock with bandaids, butterfly bandaids, gauze pads, gauze roll, disinfectant (soap), tape, scissors, tweezers, acetaminophen (pain reliever), thermometer, bee sting relief, mosquito repellent and bite relief, sunscreen, nose drops, antihistamine, a small splint, sling, ace bandage and any medications the family is currently taking. Ipecac syrup and activated charcoal are taken for some poisonings but only are used after consulting your local Poison Control Center or physician. Will you be near a phone?

Flashlight—Consider taking one for each child to use as a night light.

Bells and whistles—Bells on toddlers' shoes and/or a whistle on a sturdy bracelet for each child old enough to understand use of the international distress signal. If separated from the group, the child should be instructed to stay put and to blow three times at intervals. A whistle shriek can be heard where human voice is muffled, and the whistle does not become hoarse with use.

Matches—Keep in waterproof container and out of children's sight.

Campfires—Children must be warned repeatedly about the campfire—burning coals can lurk under deceptively dead looking ashes and cause a bad burn. No running should be allowed around the fire site, and no bare feet is the rule.

SITE SELECTION

Look for—Level sites, trees for shade or shelter if needed, proximity to bathrooms (consider hazard of crossing a road to get there), quiet neighbors.

Avoid—Cliffs, ravines, steep areas and tempting water hazards (lake, river, etc.), stagnant water

(mosquitoes). Check for nettles, poison oak or ivy, non-edible but tempting berries. Ant hills!

RULES OF THE ROAD

Never hike alone—This is not just child discipline but a mountaineering rule. Older children and adults should read about survival techniques, hypothermia and basic first aid.

Mark all camping tools—Tent stakes and lines should be tied with bright cloth or flagging, and make sure they are well placed for camp living patterns. Naturally, all axes, knives and saws must be handled and stored with caution.

Toddler supervision—Bright clothing and a bell attached to the wanderer will let you know where to look should he disappear behind a log or in a small gully. However, it does not replace the constant adult supervision needed.

EQUIPMENT FOR FAMILY CAMPING

This is a sample list to use in planning trips. Adapt it and take only what your family really needs to be happy and comfortable. Items starred are generally considered minimum essentials.

Sleeping—*Tent and/or tarp, *ropes and/or clothesline, poles and stakes, *sleeping bags, air mattress or ensolite pad, ground cloth, heavy plastic, pillow

Clothing—*Hiking boots/camp shoes/sneakers, *socks, *underclothes, *pants and belt, *sweater, *parka/jacket, *raingear and rainboots (for children), *head covering, *gloves/mittens, *pajamas, shorts, swimwear, clothespins, disposable diapers and moist towelettes, life jackets.

Eating—*Stove, fuel and matches, ice chest and ice, *nested pots and pans, *plates, cereal bowls, paper plates and cups, *cutlery, *aluminum foil, *can opener, paring knives, mixing spoon, cooking fork, tongs and spatula, potholders or pot lifter, *tablecloth, *water pail, *axe and/or saw, shovel, *detergent, scouring pads, *sponges, dishtowels, canteen/plastic water bottle, fishing-clamming-crabbing gear, *menus and ingredients, small table, *paper towels, *plastic garbage bags (to haul out trash if necessary).

Miscellaneous—Water and/or purifier, lantern, *flashlights-batteries-bulbs, *sunscreens-chapstick, *pocket knife, *first aid kit, *towels and washcloths, *toiletries, *toilet paper, *map and guidebook for area, compass, whistle, *backpack for gear and day hikes, *wash basin/dishpan, camera and film, playpen, newspaper, firewood, Kleenex, whiskbroom, pencil and pad, art/craft materials, *thermos bottles (coffee, juice, milk), pocket books on wildflowers, birds-trees-insects-stars-songs-sea life-geology, etc., barbeque grill and charcoal.

Happy camping! (These guidelines are suggested for car camping with young children. Check additional resources for moving into backpacking.)

Index